M000006657

CONTEMPORARY'S Reading Basics

Intermediate 2

McGraw Hill Wright Group

Wright Group

ISBN: 0-8092-0724-9

© 2001 McGraw-Hill/Contemporary
All rights reserved. No part of this book may be reproduced, stored in a
retrieval system, or transmitted in any form or by
any means, electronic, mechanical, photocopying, recording, or otherwise,
without prior permission of the publisher.

Send all inquiries to:
Wright Group/McGraw-Hill
130 E. Randolph, Suite 400
Chicago, IL 60601
Manufactured in the United States of America.

8 9 10 11 12 VHG 08 07

The **McGraw·Hill** Companies

Contents

Contents *continued*

To the Learner

If reading has never been easy for you, Contemporary's *Reading Basics* will help. The workbook will explain basic comprehension skills. The reader will let you practice those skills on a short, interesting story. *Reading Basics* will build your confidence in your ability to read.

Using Contemporary's *Reading Basics* is a good way to improve your reading comprehension skills. The workbook covers
- vocabulary words
- recalling information
- using graphic information
- constructing meaning
- extending meaning

Included in the workbook are a Pretest and a Posttest. The Pretest will help you find your reading strengths and weaknesses. Then you can use the workbook lessons to improve your skills. When you have finished the lessons and exercises, the Posttest will help you see if you have mastered those skills. Usually mastery means completing 80% of the questions correctly.

Reading Basics will help you develop specific reading skills. Each workbook is self-contained with the Answer Key at the back of the book. Clear directions will guide you through the lessons and exercises.

Each lesson in the **workbook** is divided into four parts.

A Introduce clearly defines, explains, and illustrates the skill. The examples prepare you for the work in the following exercises.

B Practice lets you work on the skill just introduced.

C Apply gives you a different way to practice the comprehension skill.

D Check Up gives a quick test on the skill covered in the lesson.

Each selection in the **reader** will let you practice reading. The article or story will grab your interest and keep you reading to the end. When you finish reading, you will
- check your understanding of the story
- apply the workbook lesson's skill to the story

How to Use This Workbook

1. Take the Pretest on pages 7–15. Check your answers with the Answer Key on page 16. Refer to the Evaluation Chart on page 16 to find which skills you need to work on.

2. Take each four-page lesson one at a time. Ask your teacher for help with any problems you have.

3. Use the Answer Key, which begins on page 245, to correct your answers after each exercise.

4. At the end of each unit, complete the Unit Review and Unit Assessment. These will check your progress. After the Unit Assessment, your teacher may want to discuss your answers with you.

5. At the end of some lessons, you will see a note about a selection in the *Reading Basics* reader. Take a break from the workbook and read the story or article. Answer the comprehension questions and the skill questions at the end of the story.

6. After you have finished all five units, take the Posttest on pages 237–243. Check your answers on page 244. Then discuss your progress with your teacher.

Pretest

Circle the word that is spelled correctly and best completes each sentence.

1. When he fell, he skinned the _____ on his hand.
   A nuckels
   B knuckles
   C knuckels
   D nuckles

2. The parents of the sick child had many _____.
   F worries
   G worrys
   H wories
   J worryies

3. Del ate the _____ pizza by himself.
   A whol
   B hol
   C whole
   D whoal

4. _____ never ridden in a helicopter.
   F Ive
   G I'hve
   H I'hav
   J I've

Circle the answer that is a synonym for the underlined word.

5. silly idea
   A practical
   B foolish
   C serious
   D inspired

6. shouted in rage
   F bellowed
   G whispered
   H cheered
   J taunted

7. relaxed all afternoon
   A slept
   B worked
   C stood
   D rested

8. additional work
   F interesting
   G less
   H intense
   J more

9. ramble through the woods
   A run
   B climb
   C jog
   D wander

10. murky cave
   F large
   G dark
   H cheerful
   J narrow

Pretest *continued*

Circle the answer that is an antonym for the underlined word.

11. <u>interesting</u> speaker
    A charming
    B delightful
    C boring
    D knowledgeable

12. oppressively <u>humid</u> weather
    F windy
    G dry
    H pleasant
    J warm

13. <u>master</u> of the castle
    A servant
    B owner
    D tenant
    D landlord

14. <u>genuine</u> leather
    F authentic
    G natural
    H real
    J fake

15. <u>mark</u> the answer
    A write
    B draw
    C erase
    D color

16. <u>general</u> information
    F common
    G specific
    H widespread
    J unlimited

Circle the answer to each question.

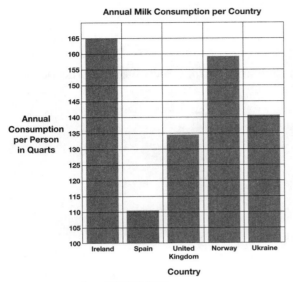

17. In which country do the people drink the greatest amount of milk?

    A Spain

    B Norway

    C Ireland

    D Ukraine

18. The annual consumption of milk in Iceland is 161 quarts per person. This is most similar to the consumption of milk in which country?

    F Norway

    G United Kingdom

    H Ukraine

    J Spain

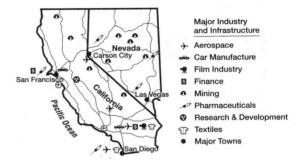

19. Which of the following is *not* a major industry in San Diego?

    A aerospace

    B textiles

    C pharmaceuticals

    D film industry

20. What is a major industry in northern Nevada?

    F finance

    G mining

    H research and development

    J car manufacture

21. Which word matches this pronunciation? (rap′chər)

   A rapture

   B rapper

   C rascal

   D rapid

22. If the guide words on a dictionary page are *guardian* and *gusto,* which word would be found on the page?

   F gutter

   G guitar

   H guzzle

   J grumpy

23. Which words are *not* in alphabetical order?

   A blank, blare, blast, bleak

   B clamor, cleanser, clinic, cluster

   C deafen, deceit, decay, degree

   D eldest, electric, element, elephant

Index

Atmosphere

   Exosphere, 126

   Mesosphere, 126

   Thermosphere, 127

Hurricane, 335

Rainbow, 411

Sunset, 478

Tornado, 520

Water Cycle, 600

Weather Balloon, 644

24. What two entries give information about violent storms?

   F Hurricane and Tornado

   G Exosphere and Thermosphere

   H Rainbow and Sunset

   J Water Cycle and Weather Balloon

25. On what page would you find information about rainbows?

   A 520

   B 411

   C 126

   D 478

26. All of the following information about a particular book can be found on its card in the card catalog except

    F the number of pages

    G the date of publication

    H names of other books by the author

    J the call number

27. The words in a glossary are arranged

    A by order of appearance in the book

    B by length of the word

    C in alphabetical order

    D any way the author chooses

28. Which information would *not* be found on a magazine subscription form?

    F number of issues

    G name of magazine

    H number of pages in an issue

    J name of subscriber

29. Which abbreviation would *not* appear on a license application?

    A FL

    B DOB

    C UFO

    D IL

30. What information might be requested in applying for a job *and* renting an apartment?

    F educational background

    G references

    H checking account number

    J hours available

31. Which of the following is *not* an employee benefit?

    A medical

    B salary

    C dental

    D paid vacation

Sneezes spread germs. But most people don't know the other hazards of sneezing. For instance, people who sneeze a lot because of an allergy or cold can be dangerous drivers. Each sneeze takes all of a person's attention for about 15 seconds. For those 15 seconds, a sneezing driver can't pay attention to the road. On the highway, a car can travel more than the length of a football field in 15 seconds. An accident can happen within those 400 feet because the driver can't see the road.

32. The word *hazards* means

   A benefits

   B dangers

   C results

   D chances

33. From this paragraph, you can conclude that people who have bad colds should

   F stay out of cars

   G let someone else drive

   H let someone else sneeze

   J not sneeze when they are riding in a car

34. What is the main idea of this paragraph?

   A Every sneeze takes up a person's attention for 15 seconds.

   B Sneezing is always hazardous.

   C It is a good idea to stay out of car if you have a cold or allergy.

   D It can be dangerous to sneeze while driving.

Many gourmet cooks prefer white pepper to black pepper because it has a milder flavor. Pepper plants bear small green berries that are picked just as they turn a ripe reddish yellow. To make black pepper, the berries, or peppercorns, are washed and dried in the sun. The berries' skins turn dark brown or black as they dry. Then the pepper is ground and packaged for sale. White pepper comes from the same berries. However, the bitter outer coverings of the picked berries are softened for a few days and then removed by washing and rubbing or trampling the berries. The skinned berries are then spread in the sun to dry.

35. Pepper plants are picked

   F   when they bear small green berries

   G   when the skins turn dark brown or black

   H   on a sunny day so they can be dried

   J   just as the berries start to turn reddish-yellow

36. Why does white pepper have a milder flavor?

   A   White pepper plants are picked sooner than black pepper plants.

   B   White peppercorns are washed and black peppercorns are not.

   C   White pepper comes from peppercorns from which the bitter skin has been removed.

   D   not stated

37. The author's purpose in this paragraph is to

   F   explain to the reader how black pepper and white pepper are made

   G   inform the reader about the best way to grow pepper plants

   H   persuade the reader that white pepper is better than black pepper

   J   tell a story about how gourmet cooks use pepper

Do you tend to spend a lot of time chatting when you make a phone call from a public phone? If so, perhaps you should take a look at the color of the booth. Some people think that the color of the phone booth affects the amount of time that you spend talking. They say that you are likely to talk longer in a booth that is brown, gray, or black. On the other hand, you will probably speed up your call if your surroundings are white, red, or yellow. It would be safe to assume, then, that the same rule is true in your home.

38. Which of the following statements is *not* a fact?

   A Do you tend to spend a lot of time chatting when you make a phone call from a public phone?

   B If so, perhaps you should take a look at the color of the booth.

   C Some people think that the color of the phone booth affects the amount of time that you spend talking.

   D It would be safe to assume, then, that the same rule is true in your home.

39. To lower the long-distance phone bills in your home, you should

   F paint the room where you make your calls gray

   G paint the room where you make your calls yellow

   H paint the room where you make your calls green

   J install a phone booth in your home

How eagle-eyed is an eagle? To begin with, the eagle's eyes are quite large. If our eyes were of the same size-to-weight ration as the eagle's, they would weigh several pounds apiece. Our eyesight would be awesome, but we would be able to see (very clearly) nothing but the floor, since lifting our heads would be almost impossible. Eagle eyes are also stronger than human eyes. That is a great help in spotting potential meals of rabbits and rodents from high up in the sky, which is not a concern for most people anyhow.

40. The tone of this paragraph could be best described as

    A   scientific

    B   informal

    C   serious

    D   instructional

41. From this paragraph you can generalize that

    F   all eagles have keener eyesight than people and other animals

    G   all eagles are courageous hunters

    H   eagles' eyes are located on the sides of the head

    J   most people would be better hunters if they had eyesight like eagles

Pretest Answer Key and Evaluation Chart

This Pretest has been designed to help you determine which reading skills you need to study. This chart shows which skill is being covered with each test question. Circle the questions you answered incorrectly and go to the practice pages in this book covering those skills. Carefully work through all the practice pages before taking the Posttest.

Key

1.	B
2.	F
3.	C
4.	J
5.	B
6.	F
7.	D
8.	J
9.	D
10.	G
11.	C
12.	G
13.	A
14.	J
15.	C
16.	G
17.	C
18.	F
19.	D
20.	G
21.	A
22.	G
23.	C
24.	F
25.	B
26.	H
27.	C
28.	H
29.	C
30.	G
31.	B
32.	B
33.	G
34.	D
35.	J
36.	C
37.	F
38.	C
39.	G
40.	B
41.	F

Tested Skills	Question Numbers	Practice Pages
Synonyms	5–10	21–24, 25–28
Antonyms	11–16	29–32, 33–36
Context clues	32	37–40, 41–44
Spelling	1–4	45–48, 49–52
Details	35	59–62, 63–66
Stated concepts	36	75–78, 79–82
Graphs	17, 18	89–92
Maps	19, 20	93–96
Dictionary	21–23	97–100
Index	24, 25	101–104
Library catalog card	26	105–108
Reference sources	27	105–108
Forms	28	109–112
Consumer materials	29–31	113–116, 117–120
Main idea	34	135–138, 139–142
Drawing conclusions	33	151–154, 155–158
Identifying fact and opinion	38	193–196, 197–200
Author's purpose	37	201–204, 205–208
Generalizations	41	217–220
Style techniques	40	221–224
Applying passage elements	39	229–232

Correlation Chart

Correlations Between *Reading Basics* and TABE™ Reading

Reading   Pretest Score _____ Posttest Score _____

Subskill	TABE, Form 7	TABE, Form 8	Practice and Instruction Pages in this Text
6 Words in Context			
same meaning (synonyms)	3, 7, 15, 24, 35	9, 12, 17, 25, 37, 44	21–24, 25–28
spelling	See Test 5 Spelling 1–20	See Test 5 Spelling 1–20	45–48, 49–52
7 Recall Information			
details	1, 8, 23	14, 15, 30, 31	59–62, 63–66
sequence		11	67–70, 71–74
stated concepts	9, 16, 27, 44	1, 3, 10, 46	75–78, 79–82
5 Interpret Graphic Information			
maps		19, 20, 22, 23	93–96
dictionary	6		97–100
index	18, 19, 20, 21, 22		101–104
reference sources	49, 50	41, 42	105–108
forms	30, 32, 33, 34		109–112
library catalog card		5, 6	105–108

Correlation Chart

Subskill	TABE, Form 7	TABE, Form 8	Practice and Instruction Pages in this Text
8 Construct Meaning			
character aspects	10, 25	16	127–130, 131–134
main idea	12, 42	4, 8, 35	135–138, 139–142
compare/contrast	41		143–146, 147–150
conclusions	2, 4, 11, 36, 43, 45, 47	2, 7, 13, 18, 27, 28, 29, 32, 33, 48	151–154, 155–158
cause/effect	14	45	159–162, 163–166
summary/paraphrase	17, 29, 31	49	167–170, 171–174
supporting evidence	28		175–178
9 Evaluate/ Extend Meaning			
predict outcomes			185–188, 189–192
fact/opinion	38	21, 34	193–196, 197–200
author's purpose	5	40, 50	201–204, 205–208
point of view	48		209–212, 213–216
generalizations	46	24, 26	217–220
style techniques	37	38	221–224
genre	13	36, 43	225–228
applying passage elements	26, 39, 40	39, 47	229–232

Corresponds to TABE™ Forms 7 and 8
Tests of Adult Basic Education are published by CTB Macmillan/McGraw-Hill.
Such company has neither endorsed nor authorized this test preparation book.

Words in Context

Greek and Latin Roots

Many English words have parts that come from Greek and Latin. Knowing what these word parts mean can help you figure out the meanings of other words. Write each word under the correct heading and then write a definition of the word. Look each word up in a dictionary to see how closely your definition resembles the one there.

| inscribe | spectacle | microwave | astronomer |
| microscope | inspector | scribble | asterisk |

Greek Word Parts

micro- = small   **astro- = star**

1. _____   3. _____

2. _____   4. _____

1. _____

2. _____

3. _____

4. _____

Latin Word Parts

scrib- = write   **spect- = look**

5. _____   7. _____

6. _____   8. _____

5. _____

6. _____

7. _____

8. _____

Multiple Meanings

Some words have multiple meanings, or more than one meaning. When you read, you need to know which meaning of a word is used in a specific sentence. Use a dictionary to find out which meaning is being used for the underlined word in each sentence. Write the meaning on the line.

1. The contractor <u>suspended</u> work on the building until the weather warmed up.

    _____

2. A wooden swing was <u>suspended</u> from the branch of the big oak tree.

    _____

3. Earth's crust is made of layers of <u>rock</u>.

    _____

4. Lee has a large collection of <u>rock</u> music.

    _____

5. The bailiff announced that the <u>court</u> was in session.

    _____

6. A standard tennis <u>court</u> can be used for both singles and doubles games.

    _____

7. The prisoner spent most of his time in his prison <u>cell</u>.

    _____

8. A red blood <u>cell</u> is so small that it can be seen only with a microscope.

    _____

A ◢ Introduce

Recognizing Synonyms

Read this pair of words:　　lovely　　pretty
How are the words alike? They have similar meanings.
Words that have the same or almost the same meanings are called synonyms.

　　　The *pretty* garden had a *lovely* fence.

Pretty and *lovely* both mean "nice to look at."

Find the word on the right that is a synonym for each word on the left. Write the word on the line.

1. happy _____ tiny

2. boring _____ mad

3. little _____ glad

4. foolish _____ uninteresting

5. finish _____ silly

6. tired _____ caring

7. angry _____ shout

8. kind _____ end

9. yell _____ want

10. desire _____ sleepy

Write synonyms to complete the sentences.

　　　The Internet has changed the way that many people _____
　　　　　　　　　　　　　　　　　　　　　11. (purchase)

items. Some people think it is _____ to use their computers than
　　　　　　　　　　　　　12. (quicker)

to shop in a store. More and more schools are offering _____
　　　　　　　　　　　　　　　　　　　　　　13. (evening)

classes for adults. "It's _____ than I thought!" one student said.
　　　　　　　　　　　14. (simpler)

"I wasn't _____ with any of my purchases."
　　　　　15. (sad)

Write two synonyms for each word.

1. cheerful

   _____   _____

2. ruin

   _____   _____

3. big

   _____   _____

4. grand

   _____   _____

5. worried

   _____   _____

6. hit

   _____   _____

7. funny

   _____   _____

8. finish

   _____   _____

9. strong

   _____   _____

10. like

   _____   _____

C ◆ Apply

Find a word in the box that is a synonym for the underlined word in each sentence. Write it on the line.

writer	famous	pictures	liked	purchased
group	additional	funny	searched	present

1. In 1926, Alice Liddell Hargreave's husband died. She needed <u>more</u> money.

   _____

2. She <u>looked</u> for an old book that she had. _____

3. Years ago, a friend named Charles Dodgson gave her the book as a <u>gift</u>.

   _____

4. Dodgson had <u>enjoyed</u> spending time with the Liddell family. _____

5. Dodgson told <u>amusing</u> stories to the Liddell children. _____

6. Alice's book was a <u>collection</u> of these stories. _____

7. The book, with <u>drawings</u>, was called *Alice's Adventures Underground.*

   _____

8. Someone <u>bought</u> the book from Alice for $74,000. _____

9. The book is the <u>well-known</u> children's classic we call *Alice in Wonderland.*

   _____

10. Its <u>author</u>, Charles Dodgson, is better known as Lewis Carroll. _____

◆ D ▸ Check Up

Circle the answer for each question.

1. We found the bright coin on the sidewalk. Which word means almost the same as *bright?*

   A dull

   B small

   C old

   D shiny

2. I won an *award* at the dinner. Which word means almost the same as *award?*

   F prize

   G event

   H program

   J envelope

3. The child was *bashful* during the party. Which word means almost the same as *bashful?*

   A noisy

   B shy

   C funny

   D busy

4. The baby needed a *cap*. Which word means almost the same as *cap?*

   F hat

   G jacket

   H boot

   J bottle

5. The teacher *checked* everyone's homework. Which word means almost the same as *checked?*

   A enjoyed

   B stored

   C charged

   D examined

6. We fixed the *crack* in the wall. Which word means almost the same as *crack?*

   F cover

   G opening

   H blast

   J finish

7. Riding the horse made her *nervous*. Which word means almost the same as *nervous?*

   A happy

   B fearful

   C angry

   D peaceful

8. The cooks made a large *quantity* of soup. Which word means almost the same as *quantity?*

   F amount

   G kettle

   H bottle

   J pot

Using Synonyms

Read these two words: little   small
The words have similar meanings.
Words that have the same or almost the same meanings are called
synonyms.

The *little* puppy was hungry.   The *small* puppy was hungry.

Find a word in the box that is a synonym for the numbered word. Then write the word to complete each sentence.

gathering	remain	prison	performer
evil	jelly	giving	understand

1. actor   _____

   The _____ forgot his lines in the second act.

2. bad   _____

   The _____ king would not pardon the prisoners.

3. party   _____

   The _____ begins at 7:00.

4. stay   _____

   Please _____ in your seats until the train stops.

5. jail   _____

   The old _____ was closed.

6. jam   _____

   Grape _____ is my favorite.

7. generous   _____

   My grandfather is very _____ at holidays.

8. know   _____

   Do you _____ the instructions?

B ▶ Practice

Find a word in the list that is a synonym for each underlined word in the paragraph. Write the synonym on the line beside its matching number.

searched	photographs	monster	fuzzy
think	caught	sure	swear

     Does a huge sea **(1)** <u>creature</u> really live in Loch Ness? Many people **(2)** <u>believe</u> that the Loch Ness Monster is real. Some **(3)** <u>claim</u> that they have seen the monster in the deep lake in Scotland. Others say they have taken **(4)** <u>pictures</u> of "Nessie." But most of the pictures are **(5)** <u>blurry</u>. Divers have **(6)** <u>looked</u> for the monster. Maybe someday "Nessie" will be **(7)** <u>captured</u>. Only then will we know for **(8)** <u>certain</u> whether this sea creature does exist.

1. _____

2. _____

3. _____

4. _____

5. _____

6. _____

7. _____

8. _____

C ▸ Apply

Write a synonym for the underlined word in the sentence.

1.   The postcard shows <u>giant</u> redwood trees.   _____

2.   We drove 800 miles on our <u>vacation</u>.   _____

3.   All that driving is <u>tiring</u>.   _____

4.   This summer, gas was <u>inexpensive</u>.   _____

5.   We camped in <u>beautiful</u> places.   _____

6.   Many of the campgrounds were <u>full</u>.   _____

7.   During the trip we met <u>many</u> friendly people.   _____

8.   I wrote a <u>note</u> to my father.   _____

9.   He would have <u>liked</u> this trip.   _____

10. Every day was <u>sunny</u> and warm.   _____

11. The ocean water was <u>cold</u>!   _____

12. I was <u>delighted</u> to get home.   _____

13. My dog was <u>thrilled</u> to see me.   _____

14. The pictures I took look <u>good</u>.   _____

15. Maybe next year we'll go some place <u>closer</u>.   _____

D Check Up

Circle the answer for each question.

1. A new *shop* opened last week. Which word means almost the same as *shop*?

   A store

   B office

   C camp

   D restaurant

2. Everyone in the *game* won a prize. Which word means almost the same as *game*?

   F party

   G group

   H contest

   J class

3. The horse came to a *halt*. Which word means almost the same as *halt*?

   A gate

   B walk

   C stop

   D jump

4. The speaker was *hard* to understand. Which word means almost the same as *hard*?

   F happy

   G difficult

   H heavy

   J easy

5. I bought a *jar* of tomato sauce. Which word means almost the same as *jar*?

   A bottle

   B box

   C dish

   D pot

6. We *observed* the insects. Which word means almost the same as *observed*?

   F caught

   G watched

   H followed

   J held

7. We dug a deep *pit* in the yard. Which word means almost the same as *pit*?

   A well

   B garden

   C hole

   D pile

8. I needed more *lumber* for the shed. Which word means almost the same as *lumber*?

   F shelves

   G wood

   H space

   J trash

 **Read On** Read "The Holy City of Mecca" and look for synonyms to help answer the questions.

A ◆ Introduce

Recognizing Antonyms

Read these words: big   little
The words have opposite meanings.
Words with opposite meanings are called **antonyms**.

Notice how the meaning of the sentence changes.

We made a *big* poster for the car wash.
We made a *little* poster for the car wash.

Find a word in each row that is an antonym for the first word. Write the antonym.

1. low	easy	high	_____
2. question	answer	letter	_____
3. before	beside	after	_____
4. first	middle	last	_____
5. throw	catch	run	_____
6. day	week	night	_____
7. true	correct	false	_____
8. plain	fancy	dull	_____
9. close	near	far	_____
10. fresh	pretty	stale	_____
11. rough	smooth	noisy	_____
12. hot	warm	cold	_____
13. empty	full	vacant	_____
14. love	like	hate	_____
15. laugh	cry	sad	_____

B ▶ Practice

Write an antonym for the underlined word to complete each sentence.

1. My room is <u>clean</u>, but the attic is _____.

2. The dancer was <u>graceful</u>, but her partner was _____.

3. The air was <u>warm</u>, but the water was _____.

4. The park was <u>open</u>, but the gift shop was _____.

5. The speaker asked the group to <u>listen</u>, but the children wanted to

   _____.

6. I <u>always</u> read the newspaper, but I _____ read magazines.

7. Turn the lights <u>off</u>, but leave the fan _____.

8. The campground was <u>quiet</u>, but the barking dog was _____.

9. The children sat in the <u>front</u> of the bus, and the adults sat in the

   _____.

10. One of the puppies was <u>sickly</u>, and the other was _____.

11. <u>Start</u> to run at the gate, and _____ at the tree.

12. Oranges are <u>sweet</u>, and lemons are _____.

13. The shirt is <u>baggy</u>, but the pants are _____.

14. The trail is <u>wide</u> at the beginning, but it is _____ near the water.

15. Years ago, dogs were <u>wild</u> animals, but now they are _____.

 **Apply**

Find the word on the right that is an antonym for each word on the left. Write the word on the line.

1. strong _____   dishonest

2. truthful _____   backward

3. add _____   pull

4. cry _____   sell

5. buy _____   laugh

6. forward _____   weak

7. thin _____   subtract

8. push _____   fat

Write an antonym for each word to complete the paragraph.

Did you know that some exercise can be _____ for your

_____ **9. (good)**

health? Occasional _____ exercise can be harmful. Some people

_____ **10. (easy)**

don't exercise during the week, and then they do too much exercise on the weekend.

But the body can't take sudden activity after _____ inactive

_____ **11. (short)**

intervals. If you want to get in shape, start out _____.

_____ **12. (quickly)**

Build _____ to longer periods of activity.

_____ **13. (down)**

Circle the answer for each question.

1. The Hornets never *lose* a game. Which word means the opposite of *lose?*

   A play

   B win

   C watch

   D observe

2. The workers were very *poor.* Which word means the opposite of *poor?*

   F rich

   G tired

   H hungry

   J angry

3. The whistle was very *loud.* Which word means the opposite of *loud?*

   A short

   B long

   C unusual

   D soft

4. Please *lower* the window. Which word means the opposite of *lower?*

   F close

   G raise

   H lock

   J shut

5. We thought the ride looked *dangerous.* Which word means the opposite of *dangerous?*

   A interesting

   B enjoyable

   C frightening

   D safe

6. The coin was *worthless.* Which word means the opposite of *worthless?*

   F valuable

   G old

   H unusual

   J shiny

7. The movie was very *long.* Which word means the opposite of *long?*

   A dull

   B interesting

   C short

   D sad

8. The glass was *full.* Which word means the opposite of *full?*

   F tall

   G empty

   H short

   J busy

 **Introduce**

Using Antonyms

Read these words: off   on
These words have opposite meanings.
Words with opposite meanings are called **antonyms**.

Find the antonyms in this sentence.

The houses looked *alike*, but the yards were *different*.

Alike and *different* are antonyms.

Find a word in the box that is an antonym for the underlined word. Write the antonym to complete each sentence.

few	after	back	old	win
funny	asleep	out	save	part
thawed	difficult	take	south	slow

1. Keep the cat <u>in</u>, but let the dog _____.

2. <u>Many</u> people bought tickets, but _____ came to the concert.

3. The lock was <u>new</u>, but the chest was _____.

4. The meat was <u>frozen</u>, but the vegetables were _____.

5. The children were <u>awake</u>, but the baby was _____.

6. First, we traveled <u>north</u>, and then we headed _____.

7. We bought a <u>whole</u> pizza and ate _____ of it.

8. <u>Give</u> me the plate after you _____ some fruit.

9. Write your name on the <u>front</u> of the form and your answers on the _____.

10. I decided to <u>spend</u> part of my earnings and _____ the rest.

11. The first act of the play was <u>serious</u>, but the second act was _____.

12. The directions looked <u>simple</u>, but the project was _____.

13. You may <u>lose</u> the round, but you can still _____ the game.

14. The train was <u>fast</u>, but the bus was _____.

15. I'll meet you <u>before</u> the show, and then we can have a snack _____ the show.

Use words from the box to complete the crossword puzzle.

right	less	high	low	compliment
insult	open	close	cool	old
young	up	down	give	take

Remember: Antonyms are words that have opposite meanings.
Synonyms are words that have the same or almost the same meanings.

Across

2. word that means the same as *ancient*
4. antonym for the word *high*
5. word that means the opposite of *down*
6. word that means the opposite of *offend*
8. synonym for the word *receive*
10. antonym for the word *more*
11. synonym for the word *correct*

Down

1. synonym for the word *cold*
2. antonym for the word *closed*
3. synonym for the word *near*
7. synonym for the word *offend*
9. antonym for the word *low*

 **Apply**

Write an antonym for each word. Then use the antonym in a sentence.

1. wet _____

_____

2. wrong _____

_____

3. calm _____

_____

4. honest _____

_____

5. cloudy _____

_____

Write three antonyms for each word.

6. dull: _____, _____, _____

7. nice: _____, _____, _____

8. cold: _____, _____, _____

9. happy: _____, _____, _____

D Check Up

Circle the answer for each question.

1. The building was very *tall*. Which word is an antonym for *tall*?

   A high

   B short

   C new

   D modern

2. The results were *good*. Which word is an antonym for *good*?

   F wonderful

   G interesting

   H bad

   J hard

3. The raft will *float*. Which word is an antonym for *float*?

   A sink

   B swim

   C bob

   D move

4. We'll *leave* at 9:00. Which word is an antonym for *leave*?

   F go

   G depart

   H return

   J arrive

5. Can you come *sooner* than the others? Which word is an antonym for *sooner*?

   A earlier

   B later

   C slower

   D quicker

6. The visitor was *polite*. Which word is an antonym for *polite*?

   F late

   G nervous

   H friendly

   J rude

7. The stamp was quite *rare*. Which word is an antonym for *rare*?

   A unusual

   B common

   C valuable

   D pretty

8. Airfare was *expensive*. Which word is an antonym for *expensive*?

   F cheap

   G costly

   H unusual

   J helpful

Read On Read "The Death of Smallpox." Find synonyms and antonyms that answer the questions.

Recognizing Context Clues

Sometimes a sentence may have a word that you do not know.

> Because Dan is *perpetually* late, we always have to wait for him.

You can use other words in the sentence to help you figure out the meaning of *perpetually*. The **context,** or surrounding words, gives you clues about the meaning of the unknown word.

Context clues help you guess that *perpetually* means "always."

Find clue words in the sentences that help you understand the meaning of the underlined word. Write the meaning of the word.

1. Many things make America <u>unique</u>, or one-of-a-kind.

   Meaning of *unique:* _____

2. For one thing, Americans are <u>diverse</u> since they come from many different countries.

   Meaning of *diverse:* _____

3. Many Americans still practice <u>customs</u>, that is, ways of living, that they learned in their countries of birth.

   Meaning of *customs:* _____

4. Many <u>immigrants</u> first came to New York, and the newcomers often settled there.

   Meaning of *immigrants:* _____

5. Today California is a <u>bustling</u> entry point, almost as busy as New York used to be.

   Meaning of *bustling:* _____

B ▸ Practice

Sometimes words in a nearby sentence will give you clues about a word's meaning.

> Saul Steinberg used bags to create *elaborate* masks.
> These decorated masks became famous.

The word *decorated* is a synonym for *elaborate*.

Find a word in the second sentence that is a synonym for the underlined word in the first sentence. Write the meaning of the underlined word.

1. Few things are more <u>functional</u> than a paper bag. They are useful in many ways.

   Meaning of *functional*: _____

2. Americans <u>consume</u> about 40 billion paper bags a year. They use up bags every day.

   Meaning of *consume*: _____

3. Today, the paper bag is almost <u>indispensable</u>. It is necessary in almost every home.

   Meaning of *indispensable*: _____

4. Machines are used to <u>produce</u> paper bags. Earlier, bags were made by hand with V-shaped bottoms.

   Meaning of *produce*: _____

5. The <u>population</u> kept growing. More people began shopping in supermarkets.

   Meaning of *population*: _____

6. Later, paper bags had pleats that <u>allowed</u> them to be opened quickly. These folds also let the bags be stacked neatly.

   Meaning of *allowed*: _____

C ▸ Apply

Use context clues to figure out the meaning of the underlined word. Write the word's meaning.

1. We heard the cows <u>bellow</u>. Their cries woke us up.

    Meaning of *bellow:* _____

2. The <u>bold</u> horse ran up the hill. The others followed their brave leader.

    Meaning of *bold:* _____

3. The meeting seemed to be falling into <u>chaos</u>, but then the president stopped the disorder by pounding the gavel.

    Meaning of *chaos:* _____

4. There will soon be <u>festivities</u>. The parties will start when the guests arrive.

    Meaning of *festivities:* _____

5. <u>Drenched</u> by the rain storm, we changed our soaked clothes.

    Meaning of *drenched:* _____

6. I knew that the fever made me look <u>flushed</u>. I could feel my face turn red.

    Meaning of *flushed:* _____

7. The winter was especially <u>harsh</u>. The rough weather made the winter seem very long.

    Meaning of *harsh:* _____

8. The <u>image</u> of my dog came into my mind. I could picture exactly how he looked.

    Meaning of *image:* _____

9. The rafting trip was <u>hazardous</u>. No one had told me it would be so dangerous.

    Meaning of *hazardous:* _____

10. The book of riddles was <u>inane</u>, but I enjoyed it because I like foolish things sometimes.

    Meaning of *inane:* _____

Read each selection and use context clues to answer the questions. Then circle the correct answer.

1. Earth's temperature does <u>fluctuate</u>. These changes in climate are caused by the changes in the speed of the turning planet. Some scientists believe the temperature will continue to get warmer.

   To *fluctuate* means to

   A predict

   B change

   C turn

   D travel

2. The Aztecs had ideas about education. At age three, children were <u>assigned</u> the tasks of weaving and <u>grinding</u> grain. As they grew older, they were given other jobs, such as fishing and making cloth.

   Tasks were *assigned* means that the children

   F did not have work to do

   G were not able to do the work

   H had jobs given to them

   J helped each other with work

3. The general wore gold <u>epaulets</u> on the shoulders of his good <u>uniform</u>.

   Epaulets are

   A belts

   B gold dress shoes

   C golden necklaces

   D fancy shoulder pads

4. Years ago, people tried to catch lobsters with a long pole with a hook on the end. Today, lobster fishers no longer use this old, <u>outmoded</u> method. They now set traps that are cages with openings.

   Something that is *outmoded* is

   F old-fashioned

   G popular

   H illegal

   J new

5. In tests, Jeff usually goes with his <u>initial</u> answer since his first idea is often correct.

   Another word for *initial* is

   A second

   B only

   C first

   D last

6. Tia's <u>flaxen</u> hair shown like gold in the sunlight.

   Another word for *flaxen* is

   F blonde

   G dirty

   H short

   J curly

Using Context Clues

Sometimes you can use words or phrases in a passage to figure out the meaning of a word. These context clues can help you.

Seaweed provides homes for millions of creatures.
In the ocean, seaweed **hosts** fish and crabs.

In the first sentence, the phrase *provides homes* helps you to know that *hosts* means "provides a living place for."

Read the passage. Using context clues, circle the answer to each question.

All green plants <u>manufacture</u> their own food. They make food by <u>combining</u>, or joining, soil nutrients, water, and sunlight. But some other plants don't make their own food. They are <u>incapable</u> of using sunlight to make food. They live off other plants that do. However, these plants are necessary. They help in the <u>decomposition</u> of dead and dying plants. That breakdown is an important stage in nature's life and death.

1. What does *manufacture* mean?

make   eat

2. What does *combining* mean?

joining   taking apart

3. What does *incapable* mean?

able   not able

4. What does *decomposition* mean?

the process of breaking down   the process of getting food from the sun

◆B Practice

Sometimes a sentence contains a group of words that defines, or gives the meaning of, another word.

Use the <u>tiller</u>, or handle, of the boat to steer.

The phrase tells you that a *tiller* is a small handle used to steer a boat.

Use the context clues to figure out the meaning of each underlined word. Write the meaning of the word.

1. Don't step on the <u>thistles</u>, or prickly weeds.

   _____

2. This year we learned about <u>taxonomy</u>, the groupings of plants and animals.

   _____

3. A <u>snorkel</u>, or breathing tube, can help you swim underwater.

   _____

4. Look for fruit that is <u>ripe</u>, or ready to eat.

   _____

5. The <u>preface</u>, the introduction to the book, is very short.

   _____

6. The choir sang a <u>medley</u>—several tunes one after the other.

   _____

7. A <u>lighthouse</u>, or tall tower with a bright light, warns sailors of dangers.

   _____

8. The sign told us we might encounter <u>gnats</u>—small, biting flies.

   _____

C ▶ Apply

Use context clues to figure out the meanings of the underlined words. Remember, the context includes the entire paragraph. Write a definition of each word on the line with the matching number.

Fashions of the 1930s **(1)** varied, or changed, greatly from those of the 1920s. Women began to **(2)** mimic, or copy, the styles of Hollywood movie stars. Bangle bracelets, necklaces, and earrings came into **(3)** vogue. Women enjoyed wearing **(4)** entrancing, that is, fascinating hats. Shoulder pads made shoulders seem bigger while they **(5)** minimized waists. Evening gowns had **(6)** flounces, or pleated strips of cloth, at the knee. As for **(7)** footwear, the demand was for high-heeled shoes.

1. _____

2. _____

3. _____

4. _____

5. _____

6. _____

7. _____

Read each selection and circle the answer for each question.

The lyrics, or words, to the song "Home, Sweet Home" were written by a man named John Howard Payne. Oddly, he was a transient person all of his life. He moved about and never had a place to call home.

1. *Lyrics* are
   - **A** homeless people
   - **B** words to a song
   - **C** notes to a melody
   - **D** dance steps

2. A *transient* person
   - **F** stays in one place
   - **G** writes words to songs
   - **H** travels and doesn't settle down
   - **J** has one home

The ostrich is a funny-looking bird. But male ostriches can be dangerous. When they are looking for a mate, anyone can provoke their anger. They kick enemies with their long legs.

3. The *ostrich* is a
   - **A** bird
   - **B** dog
   - **C** mate
   - **D** fish

4. To *provoke* means to
   - **F** slow down
   - **G** bring about
   - **H** contain
   - **J** put together

Frederic Remington was an adventurer who set out for the American frontier in the 1880s. He left New York to explore the West as a cowboy and sheep rancher. Those years served as inspiration for his art for the rest of his life.

5. The *frontier* is
   - **A** a home
   - **B** a boat
   - **C** an unknown area
   - **D** a group of animals

6. An *inspiration* is
   - **F** a railroad
   - **G** music
   - **H** education
   - **J** creative thought

Read On   As you read "Josephine Baker: The Toast of Paris," use context clues to understand unfamiliar words. Then answer the questions.

A ▶ Introduce

Spelling Words

Spelling is important in your daily life. Knowing and practicing some rules will help you when you spell words.

Plurals

Plurals are words that mean two or more. Most plurals are formed by adding -s.

    bird   birds   flower   flowers

When a word ends in *s, ss, sh, ch,* or *x,* add -*es* to form the plural.

    dress   dress**es**   box   box**es**

When a word ends in a consonant followed by *y,* change the *y* to *i* and add -*es.*

    penny   penn**ies**   ferry   ferr**ies**

Consonant Pairs

Two consonants can stand for one sound.

    shine   **th**in   **wh**ite

Silent Consonants

Some words have consonants that you do not hear.

    wrap   **k**not   si**g**n

Follow the rules for forming plurals. Write the words.

1. bat   batch   baby

   _____   _____   _____

2. branch   bottle   lobby

   _____   _____   _____

3. body   grass   bed

   _____   _____   _____

4. desk   canary   bush

   _____   _____   _____

Add *sh*, *th*, or *wh* to make a word. Write the word in the sentence.

1. ____hape

   I made the gelatin in the _____ of a fish.

2. ____under

   My dog is afraid of _____.

3. ____eel

   The _____ on the car was broken.

4. ____irsty

   We were very _____ after our walk.

5. ____ale

   The _____ is one of the largest mammals.

6. ____eets

   Put the clean _____ in the closet.

7. ____ine

   The puppy began to _____ when we left.

8. ____ips

   Three large _____ were docked in the harbor.

9. ____istle

   Come to the gate when you hear my _____.

10. ____irty

    _____ people came to the movie.

11. ____arks

    _____ are known for their sharp teeth.

12. ____ick

    The _____ book made my backpack very heavy.

C ▶ Apply

Write each word from the box next to its definition. Circle the silent consonant.

knee	scent	knock	sign	wrap
scene	gnome	knot	write	wren

1. an act in a play _____

2. smell _____

3. write one's name _____

4. small songbird _____

5. small, imaginary person _____

6. cover something up _____

7. put words on paper _____

8. hit repeatedly _____

9. string tied together _____

10. middle joint of a leg _____

Circle the answer for each question.

1. Which word is spelled correctly?

   A windows

   B windowss

   C windowes

   D windowws

2. Which word is spelled correctly?

   F batchs

   G batches

   H batchess

   J batchss

3. Which word is spelled correctly?

   A shhirt

   B sshirt

   C shirt

   D shirtt

4. Which word is spelled correctly?

   F lunchs

   G lunches

   H lunchss

   J lunchess

5. Which word is spelled correctly?

   A shhape

   B shape

   C sshape

   D shappe

6. Which word is spelled correctly?

   F knock

   G nock

   H knok

   J nok

7. Which word is spelled correctly?

   A wist

   B wrist

   C rist

   D wrrist

8. Which word is spelled correctly?

   F berryies

   G berrys

   H berries

   J berris

9. Which word is spelled correctly?

   A papers

   B paperss

   C paperes

   D paperies

10. Which word is spelled correctly?

    F babis

    G babys

    H babies

    J babyies

A Introduce

Spelling Words

Knowing how to spell words correctly will help you share your thoughts and ideas with others. Learning spelling rules can make it easier for you to spell correctly.

Comparisons

Comparative forms of adjectives are made by adding *er* and *est*.

| tall | tall**er** | tall**est** |
| short | short**er** | short**est** |

Sometimes you have to double a final consonant or change a *y* to an *i* before adding the ending.

| hot | hot**ter** | hot**test** |
| pretty | prett**ier** | prett**iest** |

Compound Words

When two small words are joined together to form one word, they make a **compound word**.

| rain + bow | back + pack | water + melon |
| rainbow | backpack | watermelon |

Contractions

A contraction is a short way to write two words. An apostrophe (') takes the place of some letters.

| I have | **I've** | is not | **isn't** |

Spell the following words using the rules listed above.

1. big + -est _____

2. happy + -er _____

3. heavy + -est _____

4. camp + ground _____

5. fire + fly _____

6. can + not _____

7. I + am _____

B ▶ Practice

Combine a word from List A and a word from List B to make a compound word. Write the words. Then use the words to complete the sentences below.

List A	List B	
water	chair	_____
arm	light	_____
flash	cake	_____
camp	berry	_____
cup	paper	_____
bed	case	_____
every	ground	_____
straw	room	_____
news	thing	_____
suit	proof	_____

1. The _____ and the sofa are covered in blue corduroy.

2. My favorite kind of pie is _____.

3. The _____ had a report on the fire.

4. She brought _____ we needed for the party.

5. Let's put the desk in the _____.

6. The _____ had grills and picnic tables.

7. The _____ needs new batteries.

8. I packed my clothes in the small _____.

9. I need a _____ jacket to wear in the rain.

10. The _____ had extra frosting.

Match each phrase with its contraction. Write the contraction on the line. Then use some of the contractions to complete the paragraph below.

1. I have _____   what's

2. would not _____   couldn't

3. what is _____   wouldn't

4. it is _____   can't

5. there is _____   I've

6. could not _____   didn't

7. I am _____   I'm

8. cannot _____   there's

9. did not _____   it's

10. she had _____   she'd

I think **(11)** _____ nothing more enjoyable than

planning a vacation. But I **(12)** _____ decide where

I want to go this year. **(13)** _____ thinking of taking

a biking trip. **(14)** _____ always wanted to try one.

My friend Alison went on a biking trip in California last year. She

(15) _____ have any complaints!

D ▶ Check Up

Circle the answer for each question.

1. Which word is spelled correctly?
    A smaller
    B smallr
    C smaler
    D smallerr

2. Which word is spelled correctly?
    F bokmark
    G bookkmark
    H bookmark
    J bookmarkk

3. Which word is spelled correctly?
    A easer
    B easyier
    C easier
    D easyer

4. Which word is spelled correctly?
    F teacup
    G tecup
    H teacupp
    J teacuup

5. Which word is spelled correctly?
    A buser
    B busier
    C busir
    D busyer

6. Which word is spelled correctly?
    F thats
    G thats'
    H that's
    J that'ss

7. Which word is spelled correctly?
    A everthing
    B everything
    C everithing
    D everythin

8. Which word is spelled correctly?
    F hed
    G hed'
    H he'd
    J h'ed

9. Which word is spelled correctly?
    A slideing
    B sliding
    C sliddeing
    D slidding

10. Which word is spelled correctly?
    F they're
    G theyre
    H theyr'e
    J the're

Read On   Read "Mystery Monument."
Answer the questions and consider the spelling of words.

Review

Synonyms

Words that have the same or similar meaning are called *synonyms*.

I don't *recall* what I had for dinner last night.
What word is a synonym for *recall?*   like   remember

Antonyms

Words that have opposite meanings are called *antonyms*.

Winning a million dollars is my *fantasy*.
Going to work every day is my _____.
What word is an antonym for *fantasy?*   dream   reality

Context Clues

You can figure out the meaning of a word by looking at the words and ideas around the unknown word.

The nomads moved from place to place in search of grazing land for their herds.
What is the meaning of *nomad?* _____

Spelling Words

Plurals can be formed by adding *-s* or *-es*. When a word ends in a consonant followed by *y*, change the *y* to *i* before adding *-es*.

Write the plurals of *cannon, ditch,* and *battery*.

_____

Some words have silent consonants.

Underline the silent consonants in these words: *wring*   *knob*

To make comparisons, add *-er* and *-est* to root words.

Write the comparative forms of *thin* and *heavy*.

_____

Compound words are formed by putting two words together.

Write the compound word made by joining *base* and *ball*.

_____

A contraction is a short way to write two words. An apostrophe takes the place of some letters.

Write the contractions for *he will* and *do not*.

_____

Assessment

Circle the answer that is a synonym for the underlined word.

1. Their purple house is distinct from others in the neighborhood.
   A similar
   B different
   C far
   D patterned

2. The banquet room can hold 500 people.
   F accommodate
   G release
   H possess
   J suspend

3. The mayor made a commitment to the voters.
   A appointment
   B promise
   C recommendation
   D suggestion

4. Driving a fancy car made him look prosperous.
   F poor
   G stingy
   H wealthy
   J generous

5. The play lasted for two hours with an interruption.
   A intermission
   B interval
   C invention
   D investigation

6. The parrot mimicked the man's words.
   F whispered
   G forgot
   H prepared
   J copied

7. The prisoner was sentenced to serve two years for the crime.
   A verdict
   B activity
   C offense
   D plan

8. Her science teacher influenced her to become a doctor.
   F taught
   G forced
   H embarrassed
   J inspired

Circle the answer that is an antonym for the underlined word.

9. You will fail the course if you don't complete the required assignments.
   A necessary
   B optional
   C easy
   D introductory

10. Saving the child from the burning building was an act of bravery.
    F cowardice
    G guilt
    H thoughtfulness
    J courage

11. Many families were destitute after the earthquake.
    A welcome
    B determined
    C salaried
    D wealthy

12. After the delivery man failed to show up for the third day in a row, I was <u>furious</u>.

    F happy

    G frightened

    H angry

    J forgiving

13. The sweater didn't fit, so I decided to <u>return</u> it.

    A give

    B fix

    C buy

    D release

14. Lack of sleep had an <u>adverse</u> effect on his health.

    F beneficial

    G prolonged

    H measurable

    J consistent

15. The tornado was the <u>cause</u> of much damage.

    A reason

    B problem

    C price

    D effect

16. The boss <u>complimented</u> Ann's careful attention to detail.

    F praised

    G applauded

    H criticized

    J ignored

17. The candidate's actions <u>contradicted</u> his campaign promise.

    A confused

    B coordinated

    C supported

    D increased

Choose the correct plural for the underlined word. Then circle the answer.

18. <u>bunch</u> of flowers

    F bunchies

    G bunchs

    H bunches

    J bunchss

19. red, ripe <u>cherry</u>

    A cherries

    B cherryies

    C cherryes

    D cherrys

20. china <u>platter</u>

    F platteres

    G platteries

    H platters

    J plattrs

21. city <u>tax</u>

    A taxxes

    B taxeis

    C taxs

    D taxes

Circle the correct word.

22. the <u>most cute</u> puppy

    F cuttest

    G cutest

    H cutiest

    J cuttier

23. shortened form of *he will*

    A he'd

    B he's

    C he'll

    D he'l

24. combination of *snow* and *storm*

    F snowestorm

    G snowball

    H snowplow

    J snowstorm

25. road that is not as long as another

    A shortr

    B shorter

    C shorty

    D shortier

26. combination of *wind* and *shield*

    F windshield

    G windpipe

    H windsock

    J windishield

27. shortened form of *I have*

    A I'm

    B I've

    C I'll

    D I'd

28. shortened form of *you are*

    F your

    G you've

    H you'll

    J you're

29. the most silky blouse

    A silkiest

    B silkest

    C silkyest

    D silkeist

Read the paragraph and circle the answer for each question.

Welding is a process for joining pieces of metal. First, both pieces that are to be joined must be heated to their melting points. This is usually done with a gas torch or an electric welding tool. The two pieces of metal are put next to each other. Then when they begin to melt, they fuse. When the metals cool, they are permanently joined together—unless they are melted again. These metals are sprayed with special gases while they are cooling. Otherwise, the newly welded metal would be brittle and could break easily.

30. The word *fuse* means

    F separate

    G bend

    H hot

    J join

31. What means the opposite of the underlined word in this sentence? *When the metals cool, they are permanently joined together—unless they are melted again.*

    A quickly

    B completely

    C temporarily

    D perpetually

Idioms

When someone tells you to "hold your tongue," he or she is using an **idiom** to tell you to keep quiet. An **idiom** is a phrase or expression whose meaning cannot be understood from the ordinary meanings of the words in it. Write the meaning of each of the following idioms. If you are unsure of the meaning, look up the idiom in a dictionary. You'll find idioms listed under the most important word of the idiom.

put our heads together   to plan together

1. hit the nail on the head

   _____

2. hold your horses

   _____

3. raining cats and dogs

   _____

4. the upper hand

   _____

5. under the weather

   _____

Use each of the following colorful idioms in a sentence.

6. in the pink

   _____

7. green thumb

   _____

8. out of the blue

   _____

9. see red

   _____

Acronyms

Acronyms are words formed from the first letters or syllables of other words. *Acronym* comes from the Greek words meaning "tip" and "name." Acronyms are listed in the dictionary under their initials.

self-contained underwater breathing apparatus = **SCUBA**

Match each acronym with the words it was formed from.

1. _____ ZIP Code

2. _____ VISTA

3. _____ NASA

4. _____ AWOL

5. _____ laser

6. _____ sonar

7. _____ BASIC

8. _____ RIF

9. _____ AIDS

10. _____ OPEC

A National Aeronautics and Space Administration

B absent without leave

C Acquired immunodeficiency syndrome

D Beginner's All-Purpose Symbolic Instruction Code

E Zone Improvement Plan Code

F Organization of Petroleum Exporting Countries

G light amplification by stimulated omission of radiation

H sound navigation ranging

I reduction in force

J Volunteers in Service to America

Identifying Details

Details give more information about the main idea of a paragraph or passage. Some details explain and make facts clear.

> What makes popcorn pop? Each popcorn kernel has a hard outer covering. Inside each kernel is moisture. When the kernels are heated to 400°F, the moisture turns to steam. The hard covering bursts because of pressure. The result is a great snack!

The paragraph begins with a question, the main idea. Then facts and details explain the answer. Look for details to answer these questions:

> What is on the outside of a popcorn kernel?
> What is inside the kernel?
> What happens when the kernels are heated?
> What happens because of the pressure of the steam?

Read the next paragraph about popcorn. Then answer each question.

> Scientists have improved popcorn over the years. In the 1890s, a better kind of popcorn from Latin America was crossed with American popcorn. Later, Japanese hull-less popcorn was crossed with American popcorn. Today, there are about 125 kinds of popcorn.

1. What is the main idea of the paragraph?

   _____

2. Write two details that explain how popcorn was improved.

   a. _____

   _____

   b. _____

   _____

Some details **describe.** They help a reader picture something.

> Farmhouses and barns were everywhere. Most were made of wood, painted white, with black shutters.

What details help you picture the buildings?

Read each paragraph. Write the details that answer each question.

The first train cars were stagecoaches mounted on four wheels. When longer cars were needed, the cars changed. The cars were made like modern boxcars, with windows in the sides. They had eight wheels—four at each end. They had hard wooden seats with straight backs. In winter, they were heated by a small wood stove. Light came from a few candles stuck in sconces that were nailed to the walls.

1. What did the first train cars look like?

   _____

2. When the cars changed to look like boxcars, how many wheels did they have?

   _____

3. How were the cars heated?

   _____

4. How was light provided?

   _____

Changes in design came very slowly. Springs were added to the wheels to smooth the ride. Vents were cut through the roof to draw out the smoke. By 1850, seats were made of soft leather. Candles were replaced by lamps. By 1872, electric lights provided better lighting.

5. How did springs help the ride?

   _____

6. How did vents help?

   _____

7. What replaced candles first?

   _____

8. What later gave better lighting?

   _____

C ▶ Apply

Read the passage. Then circle the correct answer for Exercises 1–3.

Are you thirsty? Your thirst tells you that you need a drink. It is a signal from the control center that takes care of your body's water balance. When you have lost about one percent of your weight in water, your blood becomes thicker. This affects a center in the brain that sends a message to the glands in your mouth. They stop producing saliva, and your mouth and throat become dry.

Water is very important in the body. It carries food to all the cells. It removes wastes from the cells. It keeps the body at just the right temperature. You can live only a few days without water.

1. Most of the details in the first paragraph

   explain a fact or an idea

   give details

   tell a story

2. A person feels thirsty when

   blood becomes thinner

   one percent of the body's weight in water is lost

   he or she is hungry

3. When the blood becomes thicker,

   its temperature changes

   a message is sent to glands in your mouth

   you stop feeling thirsty

4. Write three details that explain the uses of water in the body.

   a. _____

   b. _____

   c. _____

Read the passage and circle the answer for each question.

I was born in the town of Lisbon, Maine, on a farm that my grandfather cleared from the wilderness. Life was very different then. It was a time of hardship, but we had enough to eat. We raised grain and always had ten bushels of corn and oats. We had brown bread, johnnycakes, and Indian pudding. We killed a big hog every fall and smoked the meat so it would keep. We hiked the country fields for berries to can for the winter. Often we had 200 jars on the shelves in the cellar to carry us through the cold months.

1. Most of the details in the passage
   A   describe life on a farm in Maine
   B   explain farming methods
   C   tell what the writer looked like
   D   describe what the farm looked like

2. The farm that the writer describes
   F   was built by Native Americans
   G   was built by his or her grandfather
   H   was located on a mountain
   J   was located on a lake

3. Every fall the writer's family
   A   made maple syrup
   B   went to the fair
   C   cut wood
   D   killed a hog and stored the meat

4. The writer spent time in the country fields
   F   flying kites
   G   looking for berries
   H   building a raft
   J   baling hay

5. During the winter, the writer depended on
   A   bean suppers
   B   eggs from the neighbor's chickens
   C   jars of canned food
   D   brown bread

6. The writer's family raised grain
   F   to can for the winter
   G   to make bread and johnnycakes
   H   to feed the hog
   J   to sell on the market

Read On   As you read "Six-Legged Wonders" look for details that answer the questions.

Recognizing Details

Sometimes details give examples. These details are usually part of an explanation.

> Protective coloring helps an animal hide. Colors and patterns help the animal blend into the scene. Stripes on tigers make them hard to see in tall grasses. The leopard's spots hide it in the shade of low branches from which it jumps onto its prey. The flounder changes color to match its background. The caribou changes from summer brown to winter white.

Which two examples above are interesting to you?

Read the next passage about rats. Then circle the answer for each question.

Humans' most dangerous enemy is the rat. Rats are troublesome in many ways. First, they are big eaters. A rat may eat one-third of its own weight in 24 hours.

On farms, rats eat corn, wheat, and other grains. They kill baby chickens and pigs. City rats live in stores and homes. They run through the streets at night, eating any food they can find.

In the United States, losses due to rats cost billions of dollars a year. Millions of people have died from diseases spread by rats.

1. According to this selection,

    A rats look for food at night

    B fleas cause more disease than rats do

    C rats need little water to live

2. The financial damage caused by rats

    A is not common in cities

    B costs Americans billions of dollars a year

    C is decreasing each year

3. On farms, rats

    A live underground

    B eat corn and wheat

    C kill horses and cows

4. Rats can kill people by

    A eating all the grains

    B living in stores and homes

    C spreading diseases

5. Underline a detail in the paragraph that explains how much a rat can eat.

B ▶ Practice

Some details reveal **character.** They tell about a character's speech, actions, thoughts, and physical appearance. Look for details in the following passage, when David Copperfield meets Miss Murdstone for the first time.

> It was Miss Murdstone who arrived. A gloomy-looking lady she was. She was dark, like her brother, whom she greatly resembled in face and voice. She had very heavy eyebrows, nearly meeting over her large nose.

Do you find Miss Murdstone appealing? Why or why not?

Read the following paragraph. Then circle the answer for each question.

Leo Durocher, the great baseball manager, once said that Dusty Rhodes was the craziest looking ballplayer he had ever seen. He wore his cap at an angle. He ran with the speed of a tired blacksmith. For a throwing arm, he might as well have been using a rubber band. But Durocher knew that Rhodes could hit. Because he could hit, the New York Giants won the National League pennant in 1954. During the regular season, Rhodes went to bat only 164 times. He hit 15 home runs and drove in 50 runs.

1. Leo Durocher said that Dusty Rhodes ran with the speed of

    A   a tired blacksmith

    B   a bolt of lightning

    C   an express train

2. Durocher compared Rhodes's throwing arm to a

    A   tired blacksmith

    B   rubber band

    C   crazy cap

3. Durocher recognized Rhodes's ability to

    A   steal bases

    B   throw a ball

    C   hit a ball

4. Rhodes helped the New York Giants

    A   win the National League pennant

    B   win the World Series

    C   win the summer Olympics

5. Underline a sentence in the paragraph that tells the number of home runs that Rhodes hit in 1954.

 **Apply**

Read the passages. Then answer the questions.

Some of our modern drugs are not as new as we think. Records show that Native Americans used almost 200 plants to treat illnesses. For example, they knew the healing powers of green leaves on wounds. Native North Americans also used a substance known as salicylate (suh LIH suh late). This plant extract is the basis for aspirin today. For cramps, they used tea made from mint. The juices of crushed wintergreen leaves were used for muscle massages.

1. The main idea of the passage is that

   A Native Americans used plants to treat illnesses

   B modern drugs are not as good as Native American plants for curing illness

   C green leaves heal wounds

2. Write three details that give examples to support the main idea.

   a. _____

   b. _____

   c. _____

I couldn't help but be nervous when the teacher walked into the classroom. She carried a big briefcase that was overflowing with papers. Her long hair was pulled back, giving her a no-nonsense look. She stood at the front of the class, not smiling, but looking at each of us, one by one. But when she started talking, my nervousness disappeared. Her voice was strong and powerful. "Starting today," she said, "your opinions about the environment may change forever."

3. Most of the details in the paragraph

   A define a topic

   B reveal character

   C give examples

4. Write three details that describe the character.

   a. _____

   b. _____

   c. _____

D ▶ Check Up

Read the passage and circle the answer for each question.

Many words that we use today began as people's names. Charles Macintosh invented a waterproof fabric by cementing two layers of rubber together with a liquid similar to gasoline. Today we sometimes call a raincoat a *mackintosh*. Captain Charles Boycott was a manager of property. His neighbors thought his rents were too high. They joined together and refused to speak to him. Today, if you refuse to buy something because it is too costly, you can *boycott*. John Montague, Earl of Sandwich, asked for a piece of meat between two pieces of bread so he could eat quickly. Now we make *sandwich*es.

1. Most of the details in this passage
   - **A** give reasons for boycotting
   - **B** describe Macintosh's method of waterproofing
   - **C** give examples of words made from people's names
   - **D** tell the story of the history of English

2. Charles Macintosh cemented two layers of rubber together with
   - **F** water
   - **G** pine sap
   - **H** glue
   - **J** a liquid similar to gasoline

3. The neighbors of Captain Charles Boycott
   - **A** refused to talk with him
   - **B** thought he was rude
   - **C** paid rent willingly
   - **D** made him leave town

4. Sometimes people boycott an item
   - **F** if they don't like the color
   - **G** if it is too expensive
   - **H** if they don't need to buy it
   - **J** if it is out of stock

5. The first sandwich was made from
   - **A** bread and eggs
   - **B** a piece of meat between two slices of bread
   - **C** a bagel and cheese
   - **D** an English muffin and meat

6. John Montague created a sandwich
   - **F** to use up his bread
   - **G** so he could eat quickly
   - **H** because steak was too costly
   - **J** to start a new trend

Read On   Read "Louis Braille's Magic Dots."
Look for the details that answer the questions.

Identifying Sequence

When you read a story, the order of events is important. The sequence of events can help explain how the characters change and what happens in the story.

As you read the following passage, look for words that show order such as *first, next, then, this time, before, after*, and *finally*.

One day in July of 1938, Douglas Corrigan raced his light plane down the runway of an airfield in New York. He had filed a flight plan that said he was heading back to California. A day later, the airplane mechanic and pilot touched down in Ireland. Later, the authorities asked Corrigan why he landed in Ireland instead of California. He answered, "I guess I flew the wrong way." The flight made Corrigan famous, and from then on he was known as "Wrong Way."

Circle the answer to each question.

1. What is the first event in the story?
    Douglas Corrigan left New York.
    Douglas Corrigan landed in Ireland.
    Douglas Corrigan headed to California.

2. What words tell when Corrigan landed in Ireland?
    one day
    in a month
    a day later

3. What word or phrase tells when Corrigan talked to the authorities?
    That day
    Next
    Later

4. What does the phrase "from then on" mean?
    tomorrow
    from that time until now
    for the next year

B Practice

Sometimes a passage deals with events during a long period of time. Look for clue words and dates that explain the order of events as you read the following passage.

Dorothea Dix arrived at a Massachusetts jail to teach Sunday school in 1841. She was horrified by what she saw! Prisoners were roped and chained in their cells. She started investigating. Eighteen months later, she presented a report to the government. Finally, lawmakers voted funds to help the prisoners. By 1847, Dix had traveled more than 30,000 miles to help prisoners.

In 1861, Dix was named Chief of Nurses for the Union Army. She trained volunteer nurses. After the war, Dix continued her work to improve prisons.

Number each sentence to show the order of events.

_____ After the war, Dix continued to help those in prison.

_____ Dix presented a report on jail conditions to the government.

_____ She was named Chief of Nurses during the Civil War.

_____ Dix arrived at a Massachusetts jail to teach Sunday school.

_____ Lawmakers voted to spend money to help the prisoners.

_____ Dix traveled around the country to help prisoners.

Write words and dates in the passage that helped you understand the order of events.

_____

_____

_____

_____

Apply

Read the passage. Then answer the questions.

In 1896, Charles Duryea produced the first automobile in his factory. Duryea sold 13 cars that first year. The car was on its way to replacing the horse as a form of transportation. In 1901, the first cars were made with speedometers. Ten years later, the first drive-in gas station opened.

Cars brought many changes. Dirt roads had to be paved. People could move farther away from cities where they worked. In 1914, the first stop sign was installed. Three years later, drivers saw the first three-color traffic light.

As more people bought cars, laws needed to be passed. In 1942, the speed limit was set at 35 miles per hour. In 1973, it was changed to 55 miles an hour. In 1965, the first laws were passed to limit car emissions. Thirty years later, General Motors sold electric cars.

1. How many cars were sold during the first year that Duryea produced cars?

_____

2. In what year did the first drive-in gas station open?

_____

3. Which were installed first, stop signs or traffic lights?

_____

4. What was the first speed limit that was set by the government?

_____

5. What was the speed limit changed to in 1973?

_____

6. What new kind of cars did General Motors first sell in 1995?

_____

D Check Up

Read the passage and circle the answer for each question.

In 1898, a young inventor named H. Cecil Booth watched a demonstration about a "dust-removing" machine. He saw that a lot of dust missed the box and landed on the carpet.

For several days, Booth experimented with ways to use suction to collect dust. He found that dust collected nicely in a cloth handkerchief. He patented his suction cleaner in 1901.

That first vacuum cleaner was huge, about the size of a refrigerator. But the vacuum cleaner greatly improved health. During World War I, spotted fever spread through germs in the dust. Booth and his vacuum cleaners helped end the spread of the fever.

1. What did Booth see in 1898?
   A a play about a vacuum cleaner
   B a demonstration about a dust-removing machine
   C a demonstration about cooking
   D a race in the dirt

2. What happened to much of the dust during the demonstration that Booth watched?
   F It landed in a bag.
   G It missed the box.
   H It was swept away.
   J It was caught in a handkerchief.

3. What did Booth do for several days after the demonstration?
   A experimented with suction
   B went to the hospital
   C met with other inventors
   D returned to school

4. When did Booth patent, or register, his suction cleaner?
   F 1898
   G during World War I
   H 1901
   J 1920

5. What advantage did the vacuum cleaner have for consumers?
   A It was huge.
   B It was patented.
   C It improved health.
   D It used suction.

6. Which of these events happened last?
   F Booth went to a demonstration.
   G Booth experimented with suction.
   H Booth patented his machine.
   J Vacuum cleaners helped stop the spread of spotted fever.

Recognizing Sequence

Sometimes you will read instructions that explain how to do something. The sequence of the steps in the instructions will be very important. Clue words, such as *first, then, before, after, next,* and *finally* will help you follow the order.

Read the passage. Then write the steps in order.

A chef's salad can provide a quick and healthy lunch. First, find a salad bowl to use. Then, wash and shred the lettuce. Put the lettuce in the salad bowl. Top with grated carrots. Then slice eggs, tomatoes, and cucumbers. Arrange them around the side of the bowl. Next, put shredded chicken in the middle. Finally, top with cheese.

1. _____

2. _____

3. _____

4. _____

5. _____

6. _____

7. _____

8. _____

◆B Practice

**When you read an explanation, think about *when* the events happen.
Underline the clue words as you read the following passage.**

In 1952, fog in the city of London turned deadly. On December 4, cold air became trapped under a layer of warm air. Overnight, a fog formed in the cool air. Pollutants from thousands of furnaces then entered the air mass. For the next four days, all of London was covered by a nearly black sky. The harmful air found its way into homes and offices. Thousands of people died from the effects.

Answer the following questions.

1. What happened in London in 1952?

   _____

   _____

2. What happened overnight?

   _____

   _____

3. How did pollutants get into the air?

   _____

   _____

4. How did London change during the next four days?

   _____

   _____

5. What was one of the results of the fog?

   _____

   _____

C Apply

Read the explanation below. Then write the steps in order in each box.

More and more people are adopting greyhounds after they retire from the racetrack. You can be train them to live in your home by following these steps.

First, keep your dog in one room. Check on the dog periodically to be sure that it is adapting to your home.

After the dog has gone three days without a mistake, allow it to enter another room. Continue to check on the dog. If it makes mistakes, return it to the first room.

Next, let the dog be alone for short periods of time. Start with 5 minutes, and then 10 minutes.

Finally, let the dog into more rooms for longer periods of time.

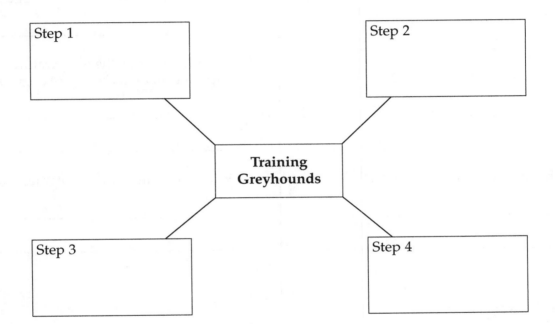

D ◆ Check Up

Read the explanation. Then answer each question.

Why does ice form at the top of a pond instead of on the bottom? The process starts with cold air cooling the water on the pond's surface. Cold water is heavier than warm water. So, the cold water sinks and warm water rises to the top. This process continues until the water's temperature becomes 39 degrees Fahrenheit. Now, as the temperature of the surface water falls below 39 degrees, it actually becomes lighter as it gets colder. Finally, when the surface temperature falls to 32 degrees, it will ice over.

1. How does the process of ice formation begin?

   _____

   _____

2. Why does cold water sink?

   _____

   _____

3. What happens to the warm water?

   _____

   _____

4. How long does the process continue?

   _____

   _____

5. What happens as the temperature of the surface water falls below 39 degrees?

   _____

   _____

6. When does the surface water ice over?

   _____

   _____

Read On   Read "Let the Games Begin." Look for the sequence of events. Then answer the questions.

A ▶ Introduce

Stated Concepts

Sometimes the ideas in a passage are clearly stated. Other times, you need to use other information to understand the ideas that are not stated.

Read the passage. Then circle the answer for each question.

In the 1800s, there were few child labor laws. One law stated that no child less than 15 years of age could work more than 10 hours a day without the written consent of a parent or guardian. But many parents gave their permission. Almost two million children worked full time by 1876. Many children worked in factories up to 16 hours a day. Others worked in the mines. Child labor was often cheap labor.

1. What is the purpose of child labor laws?
   A to protect children from unfair work practices
   B to allow children to work 16 hours a day
   C to train children for jobs

2. In 1876, how many hours could a child under age 15 legally work without written parental consent?
   A 6
   B 10
   C 15

3. Why did people often want to hire children?
   A They didn't want the children to go to school.
   B Children worked cheaply.
   C Children didn't complain.

4. About how many children were working by 1876?
   A two hundred
   B two thousand
   C two million

B ▶ Practice

Read each paragraph. Answer the questions if the information is stated.
If the information is not stated, write *not stated*.

Miles Greenwood is a hero to American firefighters. The first fire engine in the U.S. was adopted due to his efforts. It was pulled by four horses and weighed five tons. It could throw up to six streams of water. Greenwood also worked to secure a salary for the firefighters who operated the engine. They were the first U.S. firefighters to receive a regular wage.

1. How many horses pulled the first fire engine?

   _____

2. How much did it weigh?

   _____

3. Where did Miles Greenwood live?

   _____

4. How many streams of water could the engine throw up?

   _____

5. Why is Miles Greenwood considered a hero?

   _____

The tricks of Sigwart Bach remain special in acrobatic history. By the age of 19, Bach was tired of the same tightrope acts he had been practicing. In the summer of 1948, he walked on a wire suspended between two peaks in the German Alps. He crossed 500 feet of high-wire and refused to use a safety net!

6. Where did Bach receive his training?

   _____

7. Where did Bach suspend a wire for his new trick?

   _____

8. How far did he walk?

   _____

9. What other tricks did Bach perform?

   _____

10. How high was the wire above the ground?

   _____

C Apply

Read the paragraph. Then write the number of the sentence that answers each question.

(1) Doctor Frankenstein's monster has been the subject of many movies. (2) James Whale was the first director to have success in filming the story. (3) He made *Frankenstein*, starring Boris Karloff as the monster, in 1931. (4) The movie cost $750,000 to make but earned over $13 million at the box office. (5) After its success, dozens of similar horror films were made. (6) Some, like Todd Browning's *Dracula*, became classics.

1. Who filmed the first successful version of *Frankenstein?*

   _____

2. What other classic was inspired by the success of the film?

   _____

3. Who starred in *Frankenstein* in 1931?

   _____

4. How much money did *Frankenstein* earn?

   _____

5. Whose monster has been the subject of many movies?

   _____

6. How much did it cost to make *Frankenstein?*

   _____

7. Who made the classic movie *Dracula?*

   _____

◆D◆ Check Up

Read the paragraph. Then circle the answer for each question.

In the 1800s, Josephine Cochrane was a wealthy woman who gave many dinner parties. She got tired of the shattered dishes that resulted from constant washing. She finally decided to do something about it.

Mrs. Cochrane made wire compartments for plates, saucers, and cups. The compartments attached to a wheel that stood in a large copper boiler. As a motor turned the wheel, hot soapy water squirted up from the bottom of the boiler. The first dishwashing machine was born!

Soon Mrs. Cochrane was receiving orders from hotels and restaurants. In December 1886, her washer won the highest award at the Chicago World's Fair.

1. What problem did Mrs. Cochrane try to solve?

    A   dirty floors

    B   broken dishes

    C   dirty clothes

    D   not stated in selection

2. What were the compartments made of?

    F   plastic

    G   wood

    H   wire

    J   not stated in selection

3. What happened when the wheel turned?

    A   Water squirted up from the bottom.

    B   The dishes dried.

    C   The compartments turned upside down.

    D   not stated in selection

4. What did Mrs. Cochrane's dishwasher cost?

    F $5

    G $50

    H $100

    J   not stated in selection

5. Where did Mrs. Cochrane live?

    A   Illinois

    B   Canada

    C   New York

    D   not stated in selection

6. Who ordered Mrs. Cochrane's dishwasher?

    F   friends and relatives

    G   hotels and restaurants

    H   the Chicago World's Fair

    J   not stated in selection

Understanding Stated Concepts

When you read, it is important to understand the ideas and concepts. Sometimes a selection will give new information. Sometimes a new idea or word will be defined. You may need to read a passage more than once to understand the main ideas.

Read the passage. Then answer the questions.

Have you ever disturbed a mass of tangled seaweed that the tide has left high and dry on the beach? If so, you probably exposed a colony of tiny, bouncing creatures. Although they are commonly referred to as sand fleas, the animals are not insects. Their name comes from their habit of leaping into the air as fleas do. Sand fleas gather their tails and legs under their bodies. Then they straighten out those body parts with a sudden snap and throw themselves into the air. These crustaceans are different from insects in another way—they don't bite people!

1. What might you find in tangled seaweed on the beach?

_____

2. How did sand fleas get their name?

_____

3. How are sand fleas and fleas alike?

_____

4. How are they different?

_____

5. Where do sand fleas like to live?

_____

6. Do sand fleas live alone? How do you know?

_____

B Practice

Read the following passage. Use what you learn to decide if each statement is *true* or *false*. If the answer is false, explain why.

Ocean thermal energy conversion, or OTEC, is a way of changing the ocean's heat into usable energy. OTEC uses the energy to run an engine. The water that covers almost 75% of the surface of the earth absorbs an enormous amount of solar heat. The first OTEC power plant was intended to make use of some of that heat. It was built in Cuba in 1929 by French inventor Georges Claude. The plant was unsuccessful, but scientists have recently begun to experiment with ocean heat again. A small OTEC test plant was constructed near Hawaii. Other plants will be built to try to fight the energy crisis.

1. Ocean thermal energy conversion is a way to heat the ocean's water.

    true   false

    _____

2. Conversion means to change from one form to another.

    true   false

    _____

3. Water that covers the surface of the earth takes in solar heat.

    true   false

    _____

4. The first OTEC power plant was built in Hawaii.

    true   false

    _____

5. The first plant was a great success.

    true   false

    _____

6. OTEC may be a way to fight the energy crisis.

    true   false

    _____

C ▶ Apply

Read the passage. Then write five important facts in the boxes.

Maxwell Montes is one of the largest mountains in the solar system. It is 1.2 miles higher than Mount Everest. Located on Venus, Maxwell Montes towers 35,300 feet above the planet's plain level. No one has actually seen this mountain close up. However, Earth-based radar instruments suggest that the slopes of Maxwell have an extremely rocky surface. The mountain is believed to be a volcanic crater.

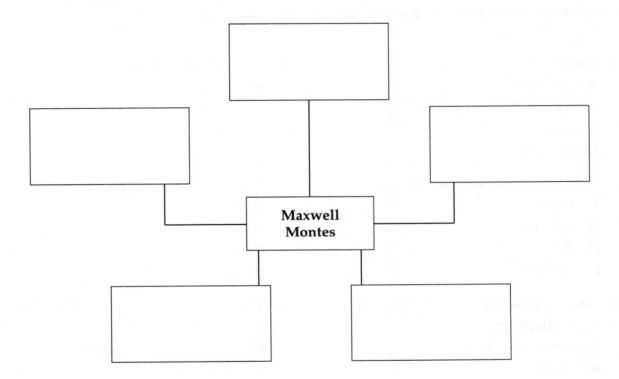

D Check Up

Read the passage and circle the answer for each question.

What we see around us does not simply flow through our eyes into our minds. The eye is one of the most complicated and delicate instruments in nature. At the back of the eye is a kind of curved screen called the retina. It receives two-dimensional images from outside. These images are flat, but they do offer information about color, size, and shadow. But it is the overlapping of the two slightly different images, one from each eye, that gives the outside world a three-dimensional look. This superimposition takes place in the brain. Without the combining of the two images, the world outside would look flat.

1. The retina is
   A the brain
   B a kind of curved screen
   C a bone
   D a picture

2. Two-dimensional images are
   F large
   G curved
   H flat
   J curved

3. The images that the retina receives show
   A overlapping
   B three-dimensional images
   C x-rays
   D color and size

4. *Superimposition* means
   F perception
   G overlapping
   H dimension
   J detection

5. Superimposition happens in the
   A brain
   B eye
   C retina
   D nose

6. The retina is located
   F at the back of the eye
   G on the surface of the eye
   H in the brain
   J in the right eye

Read On   Read "Danger in the Water: The Sea Wasp." Look for the stated concepts. Then answer the questions.

Details

Details give more information about the main idea of a paragraph. Details can be explanations, examples, or descriptions. The details of a paragraph can define, compare, or contrast.

The state flower of Texas is the **bluebonnet.** This wild prairie flower grows about **6 to 16 inches high** and is a **bright blue blossom** with a **white center.** Bluebonnets are **annual plants** that bloom in the spring. During the summer, the bluebonnet **drops seeds** from which the next year's plants grow.

Sequence

Sequence tells what happened when in a story. Authors may use words that show time order such as *first, next, then, before, after,* and *finally.*

Block printing is a way of reproducing a picture by using a thin block of wood or a similar material to make the image. **First,** the artist sketches the image on the block. Leaving the lines and areas to be printed untouched, she **then** slightly cuts away the rest of the block with a knife or chisel. **Next,** the artist spreads thick ink on the uncut parts of the block. **Finally,** she presses a piece of paper onto the block. The inked image is transferred to the paper.

Stated Concepts

One way to recall what you read is to pay particular attention to the concepts stated in the paragraph. Sometimes the information you are asked about is stated and sometimes it is not.

The horned toad has an unusual talent—**it can shoot blood from its eyes.** Horned toads are **members of the lizard family.** Their horns are sharp little spikes that grow on the top of their head. The horned toad is between **three and six inches long** and lives in the deserts of the western United States and Mexico.

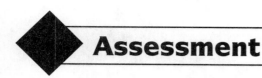

Assessment

Read each paragraph and circle the answer for each question.

If you think that guppies are the tiniest fish in the world, you're wrong! The smallest fish isn't a guppy, it's a goby. A goby is only two-thirds the size of a guppy. While guppies are common, gobies are quite rare. They are found only in lakes in the Philippines. Another difference between guppies and gobies is their coloring. While guppies are brightly colored, gobies are colorless and transparent. Since the goby is small and defenseless, being hard to see seems to be good protection.

1. If a guppy can grow to be an inch long, how big can a goby grow?

   A three inches

   B two-thirds of an inch

   C one-quarter inch

   D not stated

2. In what way are gobies and guppies alike?

   F They are the same size.

   G They are found all over the world.

   H They are tiny fish.

   J They are colorless.

When honeybees fly in a garden, they may seem to skim from flower to flower at random. Most people don't know why bees choose one flower over another. But the bees know why. In fact, when searching for flowers' nectar, they follow an exact timetable to get the most nectar. Bees get nectar from dandelions only in the morning. After that, it's time for the cornflowers. Soon after noon, bees take off for red clover.

3. When do the honeybees get nectar from cornflowers?

   A before the dandelions

   B after the red clover

   C some time around noon

   D late in the evening

4. Why is the bees' timetable so structured?

   F Honeybees cannot be away from the hive longer than a few hours.

   G Bees gather most of the nectar in the coolest part of the day.

   H Bees can only fly a certain distance each day.

   J Honeybees go to each kind of flower at the time of day that it gives off the most nectar.

Which comes first, thunder or lightning? You may be surprised to find out that they happen at the same time. We see lightning before we hear thunder because sound and light travel at different speeds. Light travels so fast that you can see lightning as it flashes. But sound takes five seconds to travel a mile. Unless a storm is directly overhead, the sound of thunder will always come after the flash of lightning. The time between the flash of lightning and the sound of thunder signals how close the storm is. If the sound of thunder follows the flash of lightning by fifteen seconds, the storm is three miles away.

5. The speed of sound is

   A much faster than the speed of light

   B equal to the speed of light

   C much slower than the speed of light

   D 15 times faster than the speed of light

6. If you hear thunder five seconds after you see lightning, the storm is

   F three miles away

   G two miles away

   H one mile away

   J not stated

The question "Do bananas grow on trees?" is a slippery one. The plant's large, droopy green leaves certainly make it look like a tree. But the tall banana stalk contains no woody fibers and is therefore not classified as a tree. The banana is classified as a plant, even though its stalk grows to a height of 12 to 30 feet. Only one bunch of bananas grows on a stalk at any one time. A freshly cut bunch of green bananas may weigh as much as 100 pounds.

7. Why is the banana *not* classified as a tree?

   A It is too short.

   B It has no leaves.

   C It has no roots.

   D It contains no woody fibers.

8. How much can a freshly cut bunch of bananas weigh?

   F 12 pounds

   G 30 pounds

   H 100 pounds

   J 10 pounds

The first mission to land people on the moon was Apollo 11. The spacecraft blasted off on July 16, 1969, with astronauts Neil Armstrong, Edwin E. Aldrin, Jr., and Michael Collins aboard. For three days, they coasted toward the moon. Once in lunar orbit, Armstrong and Aldrin separated the lunar module, *Eagle,* from the command/service module, *Columbia,* and began the landing maneuver. Armstrong chose a lowland as the *Eagle*'s landing site. On July 20, 1969, he radioed back the famous announcement "Houston, Tranquillity Base here. The *Eagle* has landed." Immediately after landing, the astronauts performed a check to make sure there was no equipment damage. They proceeded to put on spacesuits, opened a small hatch, and stepped onto the moon. After collecting rocks and soil samples and setting up automatic science equipment, they returned to *Columbia* for the return trip to Earth. *Columbia* splashed down into the Pacific Ocean on July 24.

9. What was the first thing the crew did after *Eagle* landed?

   A checked for equipment damage

   B collected rock samples

   C put on spacesuits

   D opened the hatch

10. When did a man first walk on the moon?

   F July 24, 1969

   G July 4, 1969

   H July 20, 1969

   J July 16, 1969

The Statue of Liberty, which is located in New York Harbor, is the largest statue in the world. It was a present from the people of France to the people of the United States. The statue is a figure of a woman holding a torch. The figure measures 151 feet from its base to the top of the torch. It weighs 225 tons. The torch, which the woman holds in her right hand, stands for "the light cast by the rays of liberty." The statue is made of one-eighth-inch thick copper, and it stands on a pedestal 154 feet high. The pedestal is an enormous mass of concrete reinforced with steel beams and covered with granite. By climbing the 142 steps inside the statue, visitors can reach the observation area.

11. Why did the people of France give the people of the United States the Statue of Liberty?

   A as a symbol of their friendship

   B to guide French ships into New York Harbor

   C to house a museum about French immigrants

   D not stated

12. What material covers the pedestal?

   F concrete

   G steel

   H granite

   J copper

Graphic Information

A Rich Language

English is a rich language because it has borrowed words from so many other languages. Use a dictionary to find out where a word comes from. Many dictionaries give a word's origin in the entry for the word.

> **doc tor** (dokʹ tər) [Latin *docere* to teach] a person who is licensed to practice any of various branches of medicine

Read each word origin. On the line, write the letter of the word whose origin is being described.

A tornado	**C** cargo	**E** adult	**G** grammar	**I** robot
B shampoo	**D** vote	**F** camouflage	**H** cookie	**J** lid

1. _____ Latin *adultus*, meaning "to grow up"

2. _____ Dutch *koekje*, meaning "little cake"

3. _____ Czech *robota*, meaning "compulsory labor"

4. _____ Greek *gramma*, meaning "letter"

5. _____ Hindi *chãmpo*, meaning "massage"

6. _____ Spanish *tronado*, meaning "thunderstorm"

7. _____ Old English *hlid*, meaning "covering"

8. _____ French *camoufler*, meaning "to disguise"

9. _____ Spanish *cargar*, meaning "to load"

10. _____ Latin *votum*, meaning "to vow"

A Synonym Source

A **thesaurus** is a book that gives synonyms for words. Some thesauruses list entry words alphabetically. Synonyms for the entry word follow. For example, to find other words to substitute for *alarm*, look through the alphabetical listing until you come to *alarm*. There you will find synonyms such as *frighten, startle,* and *scare*.

Use a thesaurus to find a synonym for each word. Then write a sentence using the synonym.

1. frequent   _____

_____

2. sly   _____

_____

3. road   _____

_____

4. climb   _____

_____

5. smash   _____

_____

6. beautiful   _____

_____

7. jewel   _____

_____

8. restful

_____

Using Graphs

Graphs are used to show information. They make it easier to compare data.

A bar graph uses bars and a grid to show data. The *title* explains what the graph is about. The *scale* shows how the information is being measured. The graph below compares the weekly salaries of full-time women workers in 1997.

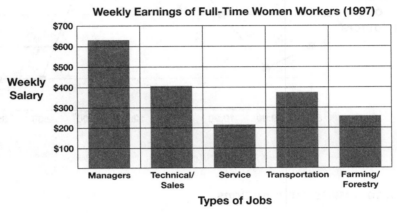

Source: 1999 Time Almanac

Use the graph to answer the questions.

1. Which type of job pays the highest salary?

_____

2. Which type of job pays the lowest salary?

_____

3. Which type of job pays about $400 a week?

_____

4. About how much more per week does a manager earn than a salesperson?

_____

5. About how much less per week does a woman who farms earn than a woman who drives a truck?

_____

◆B◆ Practice

Line Graphs

A line graph can show changes that happen over time.

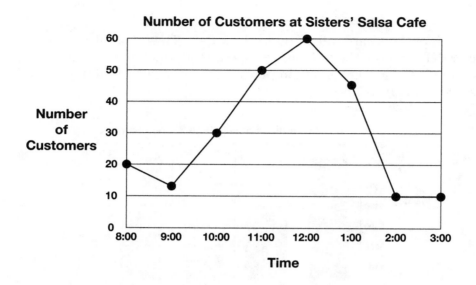

Number of Customers at Sisters' Salsa Cafe

Use the line graph to answer the questions.

1. At what time were the most people in Sisters' Salsa cafe?

   _____

2. At what time were the fewest people in the cafe?

   _____

3. At what time were 50 people in the cafe?

   _____

4. At what times were the same number of people in the cafe?

   _____

5. What is the difference between the greatest and the least numbers of customers?

   _____

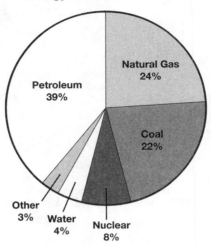

C ▶ Apply

Circle Graphs

Circle graphs show parts in relation to a whole. All of the parts together must equal 100%.

Energy Sources in the U.S.

Natural Gas
24%

Petroleum
39%

Coal
22%

Other
3%

Water
4%

Nuclear
8%

Source: Information from *World Book Encyopedia*,1999

Use the circle graph to answer the questions.

1. What percentage of energy is supplied by natural gas?

   _____

2. What percentage of energy is supplied by nuclear power?

   _____

3. Is more energy supplied by coal or natural gas?

   _____

4. Which source provides the least amount of energy?

   _____

5. Which source provides the greatest amount of energy?

   _____

Circle the answer for each question.

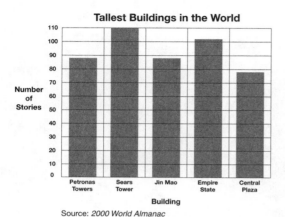

Source: *2000 World Almanac*

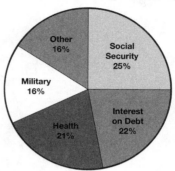

Source: *Time Almanac,*1999

1. Which of the buildings listed below has the most storiest?

   A Petronas

   B Sears Tower

   C Empire State

   D Central Plaza

2. Which of the buildings listed below has the fewest stories?

   F Empire State

   G Central Plaza

   H Sears Tower

   J Petronas

3. Which building has the same number of stories as Petronas Towers?

   A Empire State

   B Central Plaza

   C Jin Mao

   D Sears Tower

4. Where does the U.S. spend most of its money?

   F Interest on Debt

   G Social Security

   H Health

   J Military

5. Order the areas of spending from least to greatest.

   A Social Security, Military, Interest, Health

   B Health, Interest, Military, Social Security

   C Interest, Health, Military, Social Security

   D Military, Health, Interest, Social Security

A ◆ Introduce

Reading Maps

A map is a picture that shows where places are located. Maps are drawn to scale to show the distance between places or buildings.

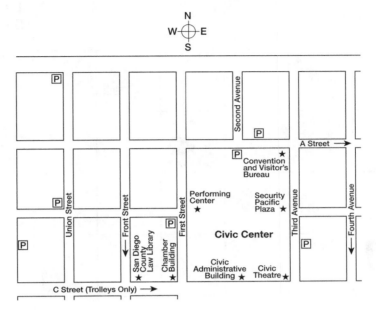

Use the map of San Diego, California, to answer the questions.

1. The Civic Theatre is located at what intersection?

   _____

2. You are at the Law Library. You walk to the Chamber Building. How many blocks have you walked?

   _____

3. You are on Third Avenue at C Street. You walk west for two blocks. What street do you come to?

   _____

4. On what street do trolleys travel?

   _____

5. On what street is the Performing Center?

   _____

The map key explains what the symbols on the map mean. On this map, coordinates pinpoint locations. For example, the Bus Station is located at B4.

Town of Waterville

Key
Subway

Library

Aquarium

City Hall

School

Hospital

Park

Bus Station

Use the map to answer the questions.

1. What does the symbol  stand for? _____

2. What does the symbol 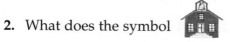 stand for? _____

3. What is located at C4? _____

4. What is located at A3? _____

5. What is located at D2? _____

6. What coordinates name the location of the park? _____

7. What coordinates name the location of the subway? _____

8. What coordinates name the location of the school? _____

C ▸ Apply

At the bottom of this map, you'll find the map legend. The legend
shows map symbols, their meanings, and how many miles one inch
stands for on the map.

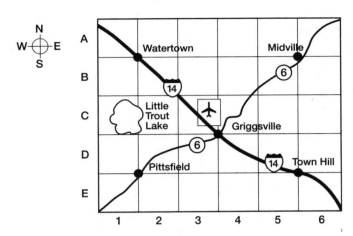

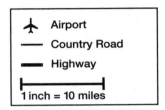

Use the map to answer the questions.

1. On what road is Midville located?   _____

2. About how far is Pittsfield from Town Hill?   _____

3. You drive from Griggsville to Watertown.
   What direction are you traveling?   _____

4. On what highway is the airport located?   _____

5. What coordinates name the location of Little Trout Lake?   _____

Use the map. Circle the answer for each question.

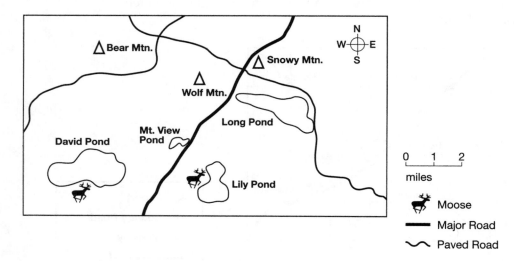

1. About how far is Bear Mountain from Wolf Mountain?

A   1 mile

B   4 miles

C   6 miles

D   8 miles

2. You are hiking from David Pond to Lily Pond. What direction are you traveling?

F   north

G   south

H   east

J   west

3. You are driving from Mt. View Pond to Snowy Mountain. What will the road be like?

A   interstate

B   paved

C   major road

D   unpaved

4. About how long is Long Pond?

F   2 miles

G   3 miles

H   6 miles

J   10 miles

5. Which is a good place to look for moose?

A   Lily Pond

B   Bear Mtn.

C   Mt. View Pond

D   Snowy Mtn.

Read On   Read "The Bermuda Triangle." Answer the questions about the graphic information.

Using the Dictionary

A dictionary gives the pronunciation and definition of words. It also gives their part of speech, different spellings, and history.

Words in the dictionary are arranged in *alphabetical order*.

To list words in alphabetical order, look at the first letter in each word. List the words according to the order of the alphabet.

If the first letters are the same, look at the second or third letter.

bet
dollar
grant

danger
dream
drip

Write each group of words in alphabetical order.

1. elephant, ant, horse

    _____

    _____

    _____

2. pencil, paper, pepper

    _____

    _____

    _____

Guide words help you find words in the dictionary. They are printed at the top of each dictionary page. They show the first word on the page and the last word on the page.

Write each word in the box under the guide words for the dictionary page where the word belongs. (You will not use every word.)

cellar	cello	lapse	convenient
lapel	lamp	convene	constant
cemetery	convent	Celtic	lapdog
cellophane	convention	larch	lanky

3. cell   cement

    _____

    _____

    _____

4. lap   lard

    _____

    _____

    _____

5. control   converge

    _____

    _____

    _____

B ▸ Practice

A dictionary shows how to pronounce words. The pronunciations use letters and symbols to represent sounds. Consonants stand for consonant sounds. Vowels represent short vowel sounds. Here are symbols that often stand for other vowel sounds.

rake (rāk)　　　write (rīt)　　　her (hėr)　　　food (füd)
tree (trē)　　　boat (bōt)　　　good (gu̇d)　　　ball (bôl)

Using a dictionary, look up the pronunciations for these words. Write the pronunciations.

1. boot _____

2. heard _____

3. strike _____

4. crawl _____

5. clean _____

Match the words and pronunciations. Use a dictionary if you need to.

6. (bom)　　　　　bail

7. (ka shir´)　　　giraffe

8. (kru̇k)　　　　bomb

9. (i vād´)　　　　laugh

10. (hāz)　　　　measure

11. (bāl)　　　　evade

12. (laf)　　　　cashier

13. (mezh´ ər)　　crook

14. (jə raf´)　　　haze

15. (jü´ əl)　　　jewel

Apply

The dictionary entry for a word gives all the definitions for the word. Sometimes you will need to read all of the definitions to find the one that makes sense in a particular sentence.

Read the definitions for each word. Then write the number of the definition that makes sense for each sentence.

joint (joint) *n.* 1. junction between bones or other parts of the body 2. the place on a plant stem where a leaf or branch grows 3. a crack in a rock 4. (slang) a place or dwelling

1. We saw bugs near the joints of the plants. _____

2. The doctor checked my joints during my exam. _____

3. The joint on Highway 12 has great barbecue. _____

mis sion (mish´ ən) *n.* 1. an assigned task 2. a voyage of a military craft or spacecraft 3. a group of people sent to represent an organization 4. a minor church that is supported by a larger church

4. The mission was sent to South America to explain our company's offer. _____

5. Our mission was to clean up the park. _____

6. We tracked the space mission on the Internet. _____

pool (pül) *n.* 1. a place to swim 2. a puddle or small amount of liquid 3. underground gas or oil, *v.* 4. to combine resources so that others can share

7. A pool of water was left on the counter. _____

8. We can pool our food for the hike. _____

9. I took swimming lessons at the community pool. _____

Circle the answer for each question.

1. Which words are in alphabetical order?

   A beat, beet, beast, beagle

   B beef, beat, beagle, beast

   C beagle, beast, beat, beet

   D beagle, beast, beef, beat

2. The guide words on a page in the dictionary are *mechanic* and *meddle*. Which word would *not* be found on the page?

   F mechanize

   G medal

   H medic

   J medalist

3. The guide words on a page in the dictionary are *reset* and *resist*. Which word would *not* be found on the page?

   A resettle

   B resolve

   C resign

   D resist

4. Which word matches this pronunciation? (nik´ əl)

   F night

   G nickel

   H nick

   J niggle

5. Read the dictionary entry below. Which definition makes sense in this sentence? The bear retreated when it saw the hikers.

   re treat (ri trēt´) *v.* 1. move away from danger; withdraw, *n.* 2. withdrawal of troops 3. period of quiet and rest 4. safe place for people and animals

   A 1

   B 2

   C 3

   D 4

6. Which word matches this pronunciation? (hed)

   F he'd

   G heard

   H head

   J had

7. The guide words on a page in the dictionary are *glim* and *glory*. Which word would be found on that page?

   A glue

   B glove

   C glide

   D global

Read On Read "Gold Fever." Answer the questions that make use of the dictionary and other reference sources.

Using Indexes

The index of a book lists names, topics, and important terms that are mentioned in the book. Entries are listed alphabetically. Each page where an item appears is listed.

Sometimes a book has alot of information about a topic. In that case, the index also lists sub-entries.

Index

Accommodations
    bed and breakfasts, 73–74
    camping, 70–72
    hotels, 75–76
    map, 3–4
Airport, 35
Air travel, 52
Aquarium, 164
Avery Island, 235

Baby-sitters, 29
Baton Rouge, 151–152, 245–246
Blues, 183–186
Boat tours, 121

Bridges, 288–289
Bus tours, 130–131

Cajun Country, 160–173
    food, 165–166
    map of, 166
    music, 171–173
Campgrounds, 70–72
Car rentals, 99–100

Children's activities, 214–220
Cooking lessons, 200–203

Use the index from this book about New Orleans. Answer each question.

1. On what page would you find information about the aquarium?

   _____

2. If you are traveling with children, which two entries might be helpful?

   _____

3. Which two entries give information about camping?

   _____

4. What topic is discussed on page 121?

   _____

5. Which two entries give information about traveling by plane?

   _____

Some indexes give additional information.

Index

salvia (plant), 32
sassafras (tree), how to identify, 131
sea lettuce (plant) *picture*, 75
seasons
    desert, 98, *picture*, 99
    mountains, 102, *picture*, 103
    northern forest, 95
    woodland, 87, *picture*, 88
seaweed (plant), 207
sequoia (tree), 175, *with picture*
silver fir (tree), 220, *with picture*
skunk cabbage (plant), 22, *with picture*
snap bean (plant), 72, *with picture*

Use the index about plants. Decide if each statement is *true* or *false*. If it is false, explain why.

1. Seaweed is a plant.

    true   false

_____

2. In this book, a picture of a silver fir tree is found on page 22.

    true   false

_____

3. This book explains how to identify a sassafras tree.

    true   false

_____

4. You can find a picture of a northern forest on page 95.

    true   false

_____

5. Skunk cabbage is an insect.

    true   false

_____

C Apply

Some magazines give information in an index at the back. For example, this index lists recipes that would be found in a food magazine.

Recipes

Soups
Flat Noodle, 83
Garlic Chive, 54
Mushroom and Herb, 22

Salads
Asparagus with Parmesan, 99
Cucumber and Walnut, 40
Pepper and Tomato, 19
Spicy Chicken, 34
Warm Bean, 93

Vegetables
Green Beans with Chives, 24
Potato Curry, 37
Tomato with Cheese, 28

Fish and Shellfish
Corn-fried Fish, 74
Salmon with Dill, 52
Scallops with Lime, 64
Shrimp and Salsa, 38

Use the index above to answer the following questions.

1. How many soup recipes appear in this issue? _____

2. Which recipe uses dill? _____

3. On what page would you find a recipe that
   uses potatoes? _____

4. Are there any recipes that use carrots? If there are,
   name them. _____

5. How many entries use chives? _____

6. Which recipe uses chicken? _____

7. On what page would you find that chicken recipe? _____

8. Are there any recipes that use tomatoes? If there are,
   name them. _____

9. In what order are the recipes listed in each category? _____

◆D◆ Check Up

Circle the answer to each question using the index below.

Index

1. Which entry does *not* have a picture?
   A Pearl Harbor
   B Peru
   C Leaning Tower of Pisa
   D Liberty Bell

2. On what page would you find a picture of the Parthenon?
   F 130
   G 131
   H 110
   J 163

3. What is a pyramid?
   A tower
   B bell
   C tomb
   D rock

4. On what page would you find a picture of the Liberty Bell?
   F 187
   G 215
   H 110
   J 198

5. What would you find on page 110?
   A information about pyramids
   B information about Peru
   C picture of the Pearl Harbor monument
   D picture of the Liberty Bell

6. On what page would you find information about Plymouth Rock?
   F 187
   G 131
   H 215
   J 198

Using Reference Sources

Reference sources give information or tell you where to find information.

Card catalogs are found in many libraries. A card catalog usually contains three cards for every book in the library. Books are listed under author, title, and subject. A call number tells you where to find the book in the library. Other information about the book is also provided. In most libraries today, the card catalog is stored on a database.

NP
4332
.S5
	Sharp, Alyssa, 1952
	Shaping Up: Exercises for Water Sports.
	New York: Healthy Living Books, 1999
	    252 p: ill.
	    Includes bibliography and index.
	    ISBN 0-11-863410-5
	
	1. Physical fitness 2. Exercise 3. Aquatic sports I. Title

Use this card to answer the questions.

1. What is the title of the book?

_____

2. How many pages does the book have?

_____

3. What abbreviation tells that book has illustrations?

_____

4. Who is the publisher of the book?

_____

5. What other subjects refer to this book?

_____

6. Why is the number on the left side of the card important?

_____

B Practice

A glossary is an alphabetical list of special terms or words that are found in a book. The glossary defines the words.

Glossary

Atmosphere: the envelope of air that surrounds the earth, held by the pull of gravity

Barometer: an instrument that measures atmospheric pressure

Blizzard: heavy snow accompanied by winds of at least 35 miles per hour

Climate: the pattern of weather that a location experiences over a specific period

Cloud: small liquid water droplets or ice crystals held in the atmosphere

Convergence: an accumulation of air caused by air moving into the area from different directions

Circle the answer to the following statements using the glossary above.

1. The book that contains this glossary is about

   astronomy   weather   plants

2. A weather condition including snow is a

   blizzard   cloud   barometer

3. Suppose the author wants to add the word *condensation* to the glossary. It would follow the word

   climate   *cloud*   *convergence*

4. One weather instrument is called a

   cloud   convergence   barometer

5. Which of these words might you find in this glossary?

   soil   hurricane   orbit

 **Apply**

Read the paragraphs and answer the questions.

Newspapers are printed daily or weekly. They provide news, articles, ads, opinions, and other information.

Newspaper indexes are references that tell which newspapers printed articles on specific subjects. The indexes give the publication date and page number for each article. The *National Newspaper Index* lists topics from five major newspapers: *The New York Times, The Christian Science Monitor, The Wall Street Journal,* the *Los Angeles Times,* and the *Washington Post.* The index lists only articles that have been printed in the last three years.

1. How often do newspapers usually come out? _____

2. What kinds of information can you find in newspapers? _____

_____

3. Name a newspaper index. _____

4. What are two newspapers whose articles are included in the *National Newspaper Index?*

_____

5. Would a 1990 newspaper article appear in the *National Newspaper Index?* Why or why not?

_____

Magazines are printed weekly, monthly, or sometimes once every two or three months. Like newspapers, they provide news, articles, ads, opinions, and other information.

Magazine indexes list articles alphabetically by subject and by author. The indexes give the name of the magazine that printed the article, the publication date, and the page number. The *Readers' Guide to Periodical Literature* is the best known magazine index. It lists articles, stories, and poems that have been printed in over two hundred magazines.

6. Name a magazine index. _____

7. How are newspapers and magazines alike? _____

_____

_____

D Check Up

Use what you know about reference materials to answer the following questions. Then circle each answer.

1. A card in the card catalog includes

   A a short passage from a particular book

   B the title of the book

   C the birthdate of the author

   D a published review of the book

2. You can find a card for a book in the card catalog by knowing the book's

   F publisher

   G author

   H year of publication

   J number of pages

3. Which term might be defined in the glossary of a cookbook?

   A astronomy

   B cross stitch

   C field goal

   D marinate

4. Which term might be defined in the glossary of a book about baseball?

   F inning

   G trumpet

   H Congress

   J harvest

5. If you were looking for a newspaper article about the Summer Olympics, you would look in

   A the newspaper's glossary

   B a current magazine

   C under "Olympics" in a newspaper index

   D the card catalog

6. If you were looking for a magazine article written by Richard Schickel, you would look in

   F all the magazines on display at the library

   G today's local newspaper

   H under "Schickel, Richard" in a magazine index

   J the card catalog

7. If you are looking in the card catalog to locate *The Lottery Winner* by Mary Higgins Clark, you would look for

   A Mary

   B Clark

   C Winner

   D The

Read On Read "Gardening on the Edge." Answer the questions that make use of reference sources.

Forms

Throughout your life, you will have to fill out different types of forms. A form is a document with blank spaces that need to be filled in. When you fill out a form, you provide necessary information.

For example, if you want to apply for a library card, you may need to fill out a form similar to the one below. Fill in the information that is asked for.

Number _____

Expires _____

DO NOT WRITE ABOVE THIS LINE

I apply for the right to use the library and will abide by its rules. I will pay fines or damages charged to me and give prompt notice of any change of address.

Sign Full Name _____

Address _____

Phone Number _____   Occupation _____

Personal Reference _____

Reference's Address _____

Your Age _____   Parent's Signature _____

[Only if under 16 years of age]

Use the form to answer each question.

1. Did you fill in the blank beside the word *number?* Why or why not?

   _____

2. What did you fill in for occupation?

   _____

3. Why do you think the library asks for a personal reference?

   _____

4. Name two other appropriate personal references that you might list.

   _____

Suppose you want to apply for a license for your dog. Your dog, Legend, is a black Labrador. He was born on July 4, 2000, and your veterinarian is Dr. Henry.

Fill in the form with the appropriate information.

EXPIRES DECEMBER 31ST

Owner: _____   License Issue Date:

Mailing Address: _____   October 10, 2000

_____   Neuter/Spay Cert. #:_____

Telephone: _____

Dog's Name: _____   DOB: _____

Sex: _____   Breed: _____   Color: _____

Veterinarian: _____

Animal Welfare Unit State House 33 Any State 00001	RENEWAL FOR DOG LICENSING IS BY JANUARY 1ST OF EACH DOG LICENSE YEAR. A LATE FEE IS APPLIED AFTER JANUARY 31ST.

Use the form to answer each question.

1. What does DOB stand for?

_____

2. Suppose you apply for a license on January 15th. Will you need to pay a late fee?

_____

3. Why do you think the form asks for a veterinarian to be listed?

_____

4. Why do you think the form asks for the dog's sex, breed, and color?

_____

Apply

You may need to fill out an order form if you want to order something by mail. Suppose you want to order the following items from the Athletic Closet catalog:

1 pair of running shorts, item #422, black, medium, $12.95
1 tee-shirt, item #423, black, medium, $9.95

You are paying by check.

Fill in the form below.

Athletic Closet
1200 Corporate Circle
Tandem, FL 04422
1-800-000-1234

Ship to:
Name: _____
Address: _____
_____
State: _____ Zip: _____
Phone: _____

Item #	Description	Color	Size	Quantity	Price	Total

Payment

[ ] Check   [ ] Credit Card _____

                 #_____

                 Signature _____

TOTAL: _____
DELIVERY: $5.00
TOTAL: _____

Use the form to answer each question.

1. If you ordered two pairs of shorts, what would the total price be?

   _____

2. What is the two-letter abbreviation for your state?

   _____

3. How did you find the total order amount?

   _____

4. Why do you think the company asks for your phone number?

   _____

 **Check Up**

Suppose you want to order a magazine. Complete the form below.

Computer News Send me a one-year subscription for $16. Name: _____ Address: _____ City: _____ State: _____ [ ] Bill Me Later   [ ] Payment Enclosed Please allow 6–8 weeks for your first issue. Foreign countries, $45.

Use the form to answer each question.

1. What is the name of the magazine?

   _____

2. How can you pay for the magazine?

   _____

3. When will you receive the first issue?

   _____

4. What is the price for a one-year subscription in this country?

   _____

5. What is the price if you live in a foreign country?

   _____

Consumer Materials

If you want to buy or sell something, you might look in the classified ads section of a newspaper. There you will find advertisements for all types of items.

The items are listed under general headings. The headings are in alphabetical order.

> APPLIANCES
> Upright freezer, white, 15.1 cu ft.
> $150. Call 555-1234.

Match each item that is for sale with the appropriate heading in the box.

Painting Services	Hobbies
Camping Supplies	Antiques
Musical Instruments	Horses and Equipment
Computers	Boats
Pets	Appliances

1. Sea Queen 14 ft. boat _____

2. apartment stove _____

3. old glass and china _____

4. 12-string guitar _____

5. interior painting services _____

6. Cocker spaniel puppies _____

7. saddles _____

8. stained glass supplies _____

9. color printer _____

10. tent _____

◆B▶ Practice

Classified ads use abbreviations to save space. You must know the abbreviations to understand the ads.

1998 JEEP COWBOY 4 WD, AC, 5 spd. 40K mi. $11,000 OBO. For info. call 555-1234	SPRINGFIELD APT. 2 bdrms, W/D hook-up, $500/mo. Avail. Sept. 1st. Refs. Required. 555-1234

Match the abbreviations with the words that they stand for. Write the letter of the meaning beside the abbreviation.

1. WD _____
2. spd. _____
3. OBO _____
4. info. _____
5. bdrms _____
6. W/D _____
7. mo. _____
8. Avail. _____
9. Refs. _____
10. 40K mi. _____
11. AC _____
12. Apt. _____

A information

B 40,000 miles

C bedrooms

D washer/dryer

E wheel drive

F references

G air conditioning

H speed

I or best offer

J apartment

K available

L month

C Apply

1998 Carpentry	Household Help
A-1 Carpentry—Painting, siding, roofs, decks. Sen. cit. disc. Free est. Finc. available. Fully ins. Call 555-1234 after 5 P.M.	Cleaning Crew will clean your house or apt. Exc. refs. Brng own sppls. Avl. MWF 8–4. Whl or hlf day. $80/$40. 555-1234 or leave msg.

Look at the Carpentry ad. Circle the correct answers.

1. What work does A-1 Carpentry *not* do?

    siding   porches   decks

2. Who receives a discount?

    students   teachers   senior citizens

3. What service is free?

    estimates   painting   cleanup

4. What service is available?

    car rentals   financing   remodeling

5. Which time is appropriate to call A-1 Carpentry?

    5 A.M.   3 P.M.   7 P.M.

Look at the Household Help ad. Circle the correct answers.

6. What does the Cleaning Crew *not* clean?

    office buildings   apartments   houses

7. What will they show to prospective clients?

    photographs   bills   references

8. On which day are they available to work?

    Monday   Tuesday   Thursday

9. What do they bring with them to work?

    children   supplies   truck

10. What is the Cleaning Crew's hourly rate?

    $20 $10 $12

Circle the answer for each question.

1. Under which classified heading would used speakers belong?

   A Boats

   B Music

   C Appliances

   D Computers

2. Under which classified heading would a sofa belong?

   F Furniture

   G Sports Equipment

   H Pets

   J Appliances

3. Under which classified heading would a ring belong?

   A Jewelry

   B Appliances

   C Clothing

   D Books

4. How are the classified headings listed?

   F by number

   G by phone number

   H alphabetically

   J by date

5. What does *lg. rms.* in an ad for an apartment probably mean?

   A long rooms

   B living rooms

   C large rooms

   D light rooms

6. What does *$400/mo. with util.* mean?

   F Utilities are not included in the rent.

   G Utilities are included in the rent.

   H The rent is $400 a year.

   J The rent is $400 a week.

7. What does *gd. cond.* probably mean?

   A grand condition

   B air conditioned

   C good condo

   D good condition

8. What information is most necessary in an ad?

   F date

   G seller's name

   H seller's address

   J seller's phone number

Consumer Materials

Part-time and full-time jobs are listed in the newspaper want ads.
The ads use abbreviations.

> COOKS needed immed. for small
> restaurant.
> P/T morn. and eve. $7.50/hr, 20 hrs a wk.
> Exp. preferred. Will train the right person.
> Benefit pkg. Resumés only:
> Maria Swanson, P.O. Box 490,
> Any Town, TN 38621 EOE

Match the abbreviations with the words they stand for. Write the letter of the meaning beside the abbreviation.

1. P/T _____   **A** morning

2. morn. _____   **B** hour

3. eve. _____   **C** experience

4. hr _____   **D** Post Office

5. exp. _____   **E** package

6. P.O. _____   **F** week

7. wk. _____   **G** evening

8. TN _____   **H** part-time

9. EOE _____   **I** Equal Opportunity Employer

10. pkg. _____   **J** Tennessee

B Practice

A resumé is a summary of a person's education and work experience. People send their resumés to potential employers when they are looking for a job.

Resumé

Laurie Paxton
1210 Earl Drive
Newton, WI 88402
Phone: 555-1234

Education:

Present	Newton Community College Course of Study: English
High School	Baxter High School Newton, WI Honor Student, Yearbook Editor

Work Experience:

1999–2000 Newton Daily News	Worked part-time after school as administrative assistant
1999 Fancy Florist	Worked during the summer as a cashier

Use the resumé to answer the following questions.

1. How could an employer reach Laurie?

2. Laurie wants to apply for a part-time job as a writer. How does her background help?

3. Some employees ask for references—people who know your strengths and weaknesses. Who might Laurie ask to be a reference for the job as a writer?

4. How many different places has Laurie worked?

C Apply

Read the following ad. Then answer the questions.

> DENTAL ASSISTANT
> New dental practice seeks licensed assistant. F/T
> 8–4, Tues.–Sat. Med. Dental, and Pd. Vacation.
> Looking for person with high standards and
> sense of humor. Comp. salary. Send resumé to:
> Dr. Higgins, 19 Oak Street, Sycamore,
> NH 83025   EOE

1. What position is being advertised?

   _____

2. What are the working hours each day?

   _____

3. What benefits are offered?

   _____

4. Which days is the office open?

   _____

5. How can you contact Dr. Higgins?

   _____

6. From reading the ad, what do you know about Dr. Higgins?

   _____

7. What might be the positive aspects of this job?

   _____

8. What might be the negative aspects of this job?

   _____

D ◆ Check Up

Circle the answer for each question.

1. What does F/T mean?
   - **A** fully
   - **B** full-time
   - **C** part-time
   - **D** for today

2. Which of the following is an employee benefit?
   - **F** salary
   - **G** insurance
   - **H** EOE
   - **J** weekends off

3. What does *exp.* stand for?
   - **A** extra
   - **B** exit
   - **C** executive
   - **D** experience

4. What is included on a resumé?
   - **F** education
   - **G** weight
   - **H** parent's names
   - **J** religion

5. What education is *not* included on a resumé?
   - **A** high school
   - **B** college
   - **C** technical school
   - **D** elementary school

Fill in the following application for an after-school job.

Name: _____

Address: _____

Phone Number: _____

Reference: _____

Circle Last Grade of School Completed:

7   8   9   10   11   12

Hours Available:

          S   M   T   W   T   F   S

Morning:

Afternoon:

Evening:

Read On   Read "Food for All." Answer the questions about consumer materials.

Review

Graphs

A bar graph uses bars and a grid to show information.

Maps

Maps show where places are located. The scale shows the distance between places. The key explains what the symbols on the map mean. Coordinates describe a location.

Dictionary

Words in a dictionary are arranged in alphabetical order. Each entry gives the pronunciation and definition of the word. It also gives the part of speech, different spellings, and history of the word.

> **mag net** (mag´ nit), *n.* 1 piece of metal or ore that attracts iron or steel. A lodestone is a natural magnet. 2 anything that attracts: *The state park is a magnet for outdoor enthusiasts.*

Index

The index is located at the back of a book. It lists topics covered in the book and gives the page number where each topic is discussed.

Lincoln, Abraham
    Administration
        Election of 1864, 431–432
        Emancipation Proclamation, 428
    Assassination, 433
    Congressman, 426

Reference Sources

A card catalog is a reference source found in libraries. It contains three cards for each book, listed by author's name, title of the book, and subject of the book. The card tells you where in the library a book can be found and gives other information about the book. Today most card catalogs are computerized.

Forms

Forms ask for information. You complete forms for many different reasons such as obtaining a library card or applying for a dog license.

Consumer Materials

Classified ads provide consumers with information about buying or selling items. Help-wanted ads provide information about jobs.

◆ Assessment

Circle the answer to each question.

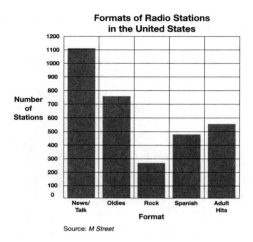

Formats of Radio Stations in the United States

Source: *M Street*

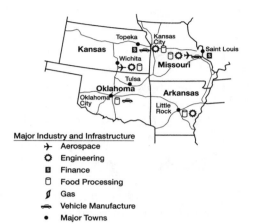

Major Industry and Infrastructure
- ✈ Aerospace
- ⚙ Engineering
- 🅢 Finance
- ⬚ Food Processing
- ∮ Gas
- 🚗 Vehicle Manufacture
- • Major Towns

1. Which format is played by the greatest number of stations?

   A Oldies

   B News/Talk

   C Spanish

   D Rock

2. Which format is played more than Rock and less than Adult Hits?

   F News/Talk

   G Spanish

   H Oldies

   J Religion

3. What are the two major industries in Little Rock, Arkansas?

   A gas and aerospace

   B engineering and food processing

   C vehicle manufacture and aerospace

   D finance and mining

4. Which of the following cities is a financial center in Kansas?

   F Topeka

   G Wichita

   H St. Louis

   J Oklahoma City

5. Which words are in alphabetical order?

    A father, fasten, farewell, fashion

    B raccoon, raffle, radius, random

    C page, pail, pajamas, panel

    D hook, hop, hoop, hope

6. If the guide words on a dictionary page are *material* and *maturity*, which word would *not* be found on the page?

    F matter

    G maximum

    H matrix

    J matinee

7. Which word matches the pronunciation (pō´ shən)?

    A position

    B poison

    C pottery

    D potion

Index

Caffeine, 126, 228	Defibrillator, 266
Circulation, 36, 66, 120	Diabetes, 216
Coughing reflex, 200	Diet, 315, 356

8. To which page would you turn to read about diabetes?

    F 126

    G 200

    H 216

    J 315

9. Where would you add an entry for Calcium?

    A between Caffeine and Circulation

    B before Caffeine

    C between Circulation and Coughing reflex

    D after Coughing reflex

10. If you wanted to learn about the causes of coughing, where would you look in the text?

    F page 36

    G page 266

    H page 200

    J page 356

11. Which of the following information is *not* found in a card catalog?

    A   title of the book

    B   author of the book

    C   publisher

    D   price of the book

12. Which term would *not* be defined in the glossary of a book about football?

    F   touchdown

    G   quarterback

    H   pass

    J   goalie

13. Which of the following information would *not* be asked for on an application for a magazine subscription?

    A   address

    B   term of the subscription desired

    C   payment option

    D   savings account number

14. You would include all of the following information on a mail order form except

    F   shipping and handling fees

    G   number of items

    H   date of birth

    J   size

15. In a classified ad, *obo* probably stands for

    A   October availability

    B   or best offer

    C   only best one

    D   only brand names

16. When do you submit a resumé?

    F   when applying for a credit card

    G   when ordering an item through the mail

    H   when applying for a job

    J   when ordering a magazine

Constructing Meaning

Similes

When you compare two unlike things using the words *like* or *as*, you are creating a **simile.**

Rewrite each sentence to include a simile. Use *like* or *as* to describe two unlike things.

The rain sounded loud.
The rain sounded *like* golf balls hitting the window.

The runner was fast.
The runner was *as* fast *as* a gazelle.

1. Tom's car is old.

_____

2. Our cat is fat.

_____

3. After shoveling the snow, I was cold.

_____

4. Swimming underwater was different.

_____

5. The noisy three-year-old came into the kitchen.

_____

6. Alex was really hungry.

_____

7. Gina was tired so she rode her bike slowly.

_____

8. The alarm clock was loud.

_____

Analogies

A word analogy **compares** the relationship of a pair of words.

colonel : army :: manager : business

An analogy is read like this: *colonel* is to *army* as *manager* is to *business*.

A colonel is part of an army the same way a manager is part of a business.

Complete the analogies below.

Part/Whole Analogies

1. Tuesday : week :: April : _____

2. tree : forest :: building : _____

3. handle bars : bicycle :: _____ : car

4. pint : gallon :: inch : _____

Worker/Product Analogies

5. bird : nest :: bee : _____

6. statue : sculptor :: _____ : writer

7. cake : baker :: painting : _____

Cause/Effect Analogies

8. happiness : laughing :: sadness : _____

9. heat : sweating :: _____ : shivering

A ▶ Introduce

Recognizing Character Traits

Characters are an important part of a story. Authors want to make their characters come alive. To make characters seem real, authors use several methods to reveal what the character is like as a person—the character's traits—and what the character is feeling.

Here are some methods an author uses to let a reader know what a character is like or what that character is feeling:

the character's appearance   the character's actions
what the character says or thinks   what others say about the
                                                                   character

Write what is revealed about the character or his or her feelings. Then write *appearance, actions, character's words, character's thoughts,* or *words of others* to explain how each character's traits or feelings are revealed by the author. You may use more than one category.

Mimi went over to the bathroom door, drew back her right foot, and kicked the base of the door so savagely that the whole frame shook.

1. What is revealed about Mimi? _____

2. How? _____

"Mother wants to grow corn in the front yard! Can you imagine what Elaine will say?" Jean exclaimed.
"Who cares? Why do you always listen to Elaine. She isn't right all the time. She just thinks she is." Paul said.

3. What is revealed about Elaine? _____

4. How? _____

She was tall and graceful. She wore a blue suit and dark glasses. She carried several packages under her arm. Nervously, she glanced at her watch as she walked down the street.
Finally, she reached a long, black limousine. The driver leaped out and opened a door for her. "Okay, John," she said. "Let's get home before Jill does. You know how impatient ten-year-olds can be."

5. What is revealed about the woman? _____

6. How? _____

Read each passage. Then circle the answer for each question.

Mr. Daley sat at the kitchen table drinking his third cup of coffee as Tom, his son, entered the room. Mr. Daley wasted no time before he spoke:

"It doesn't seem to matter to you how late you stroll in, does it?"

"It's only ten past eight," Tom replied.

"That's not the point. Haven't I told you a thousand times to set your alarm for seven?"

Tom withdrew into his usual morning shell. "I haven't been keeping count."

Mr. Daley snapped back, "The store can't run by itself, and every morning you make me late. Customers are outside waiting by the time we get there."

Tom sat staring at his bowl of cereal with the usual tight feeling in his chest.

1. What feeling does Mr. Daley show?

    A love

    B boredom

    C anger

    D lightheartedness

2. What can you conclude about the family situation?

    F Tom has no one to talk to about his problems.

    G Mr. Daley owns a furniture store.

    H Mr. Daley is very rich.

    J Tom and his father argue often.

3. What is the main way you learn about the characters in this passage?

    A through the words of the characters

    B through the actions of the characters

    C through their thoughts

    D by their appearance

4. What two sentences from the passage show that Tom does not want to talk to his father? Underline them.

It would be a fine morning, Steve thought, if Miss MacGill would stop watching him through the store window. As he pumped gas for a customer, he could see her over his shoulder always watching him.

He bent down, checking the flow of gas. There was a gas shortage and talk about rationing new customers. If he spilled a drop, she would be after him. She was always after him about something. Yesterday she had bawled him out about the air pump's not working. A woman had left the pump on, and it had used too much electricity. Steve said he would pay for the extra electricity. Miss MacGill said she would deduct ten cents from his Saturday pay. That's bad enough, thought Steve, but the way she just sits there and stares, trying to catch me doing something wrong. . . . If I just didn't need the money so bad, I'd quit.

5. How do you learn about Steve?

    F through his words and actions

    G through his thoughts

    H by his appearance

    J through the thoughts of others

6. How do you learn about Miss MacGill?

    A through her words and actions

    B through her thoughts

    C by her appearance

    D through the thoughts of another character

7. What can you conclude about Miss MacGill from this passage?

    F Steve is fond of her.

    G She enjoys her work.

    H Miss MacGill is afraid of people.

    J Miss MacGill likes to find fault.

8. Why does Steve put up with Miss MacGill's complaints? Underline the sentence that tells why.

C Apply

Read the following passage.

Emperor Flavius of ancient Rome once held an impressive banquet. He invited all the richest and most powerful people in the Roman Empire. His banquet tables were set with plates of pure gold. Their jewel-encrusted surfaces sparkled in the light of the torches. After the first course of the banquet, the emperor rose from his seat. The guests had been laughing and talking, dancing and eating, but now they quieted. "This banquet cost me a sum that would astonish even the richest of you," said the emperor. "Yet, see what little regard for riches I have!" Then the emperor flung his golden plate into the river flowing near the hall. His guests, following his example, did the same. Eventually, seven hundred gold plates were underwater. But after the guests left, the emperor called to his servants. "Pull up the nets we stretched under the river this afternoon," he ordered.

In each box, write a word or phrase that describes the emperor.

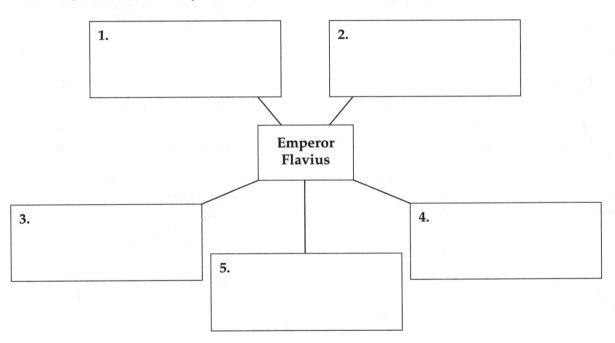

Write two ways the author used to tell you what the emperor was like.

6. _____

7. _____

D Check Up

Read each passage. Then circle the answer for each question.

John Fleming took off his raincoat and hung it on a peg behind the door. Then he took off his tweed jacket and put on the woolen cardigan that he wore at the office. Two of its leather buttons were missing. He pushed his hair back with a hand and bit the knuckle of his right thumb.

1. What can be said about John Fleming?

    A   He spends a lot on clothes.

    B   He is sick.

    C   He dresses to impress others.

    D   He is worried.

2. How do you learn about the character?

    F   through the words of others

    G   through the character's actions

    H   through his thoughts

    J   by his appearance

Kino could feel the blown sand against his ankles and he was glad, for he knew there would be no tracks. Kino could hear the pad of Juana's feet behind him. He went quickly and quietly. Juana trotted behind her husband, trying to keep up with him. They finally found the sandy road that led through the brush country toward Loreto where they hoped to find the help they were seeking.

3. How do Kino and Juana seem to feel?

    A   greedy

    B   determined

    C   happy

    D   playful

4. How is character revealed?

    F   through words

    G   through thoughts and actions

    H   through actions alone

    J   through appearance

Jeff Courtney felt very conspicuous as he hurried along the tree-lined streets of Peking. The way the Chinese stared at him was bad enough, but now he was being followed. Unsmiling boys were at his heels. Jeff tried to shake them by turning into a narrow alley but they were still there.

5. How does Jeff feel?

    A   proud to be American

    B   like an explorer

    C   out of place and fearful

    D   cowardly

6. How is Jeff's character shown?

    F   through his words and actions

    G   through his words and thoughts

    H   through the thoughts of others

    J   through his thoughts and actions

Doug Smithson whispered to me. "I think you ought to know, Ms. Larson. Don Crimp didn't come all the way to school."

"Where did he go?" I asked.

"He's up there on the mountaintop," Doug said.

"What's he doing up there?" I asked. "Why doesn't he come on down to school?"

"He's afraid, Ms. Larson," Doug said.

7. How could Ms. Larson be described as a teacher?

    A   uncaring about absent pupils

    B   interested only in teaching

    C   eager to close school for the day

    D   concerned for her pupils

8. How do you know what Ms. Larson is like?

    F   through her words

    G   through her thoughts and actions

    H   through the thoughts of others

    J   by her appearance

Recognizing Character Traits

As a story unfolds, the characters develop personalities. Writers make characters seem real in several ways. Here are some ways writers make characters "come alive":

Through narration: The writer tells how the character looks, states the characters' inner thoughts or feelings, tells what other characters think about the main character.

Through dialogue: The writer tells what the character says and how.

Through action: The writer has the character do things that reveal his or her personality.

Not all characters are people. Sometimes authors use animals, objects, or things in nature as characters.

Read the passage. Then answer the questions and complete the sentences.

"Look where you're goin'!" Eddie cried impatiently. "You're goin' in circles. What's the sense of goin' in circles?"

"That's the way the boat goes," Larry said, pulling hard on the oars. "I can't help it if that's the way the boat goes."

"Gimme those oars," Eddie snapped and pulled the oars away from Larry. Gladly Larry gave them up.

"It's not my fault if the boat goes in circles. That's the way it's made," Larry kept saying over and over.

"Aah, be quiet." Eddie pulled hard on the oars. The boat sprang forward. They finally began to head directly toward shore.

1. What words could be used to describe Eddie?

    _____

2. The narration tells me that Eddie is _____.

3. The dialogue tells me that Eddie is _____.

4. The action tells me that Eddie is _____.

5. What words could be used to describe Larry?

    _____

6. The narration tells me that Larry is _____.

7. The dialogue tells me that Larry is _____.

8. The action tells me that Larry is _____.

B ▸ Practice

Use the words in the box to identify the character trait that fits each character. Then write *narration*, *dialogue*, or *action* to tell what method was used to reveal the character trait. You may use more than one method.

helpful	impatient	brave
high-minded	friendly	sympathetic

Mr. Joseph growled at his son when Bruce dropped the jar of nails on the workshop floor.

1. Character trait _____

2. Method _____

"Thank you," said the newly elected mayor. "I will do my utmost to justify the faith you have placed in me."

3. Character trait _____

4. Method _____

"I'm sure Maria will be all right," Bonnie said, as she patted Mrs. Martinez on the back.

5. Character trait _____

6. Method _____

She didn't stop to grab her robe or purse. She knew the smoke would be in the children's room by now and she had to act fast to get everyone out safely.

7. Character trait _____

8. Method _____

"This is going to be hard," Keesha said, "but I have to help Mrs. Jefferson into the car so she can get to the doctor and get the medicine she needs."

9. Character trait _____

10. Method _____

Mr. Arnold shook the hand of the visitor and welcomed him to his office with a broad smile.

11. Character trait _____

12. Method _____

Apply

Read each passage. Then answer each question.

In the last week before the young seal was born, its mother was alone most of the time. As she swam under the ice pack, she had much on her mind. It was up to her to explore beneath the thicker ice. She must hunt for chinks in the ice through which she could make some new exit holes. She had her own places through which she could come and go, but they were too far apart for a cub with small lungs. The cub would need to rise more often for a breath and to rest on the surface. When the female found a place that seemed right, she began breathing on the underside of the ice. As it softened, she nibbled and clawed at it, forming the first tunnel to the surface.

1. Who is the main character in this passage? _____

2. What two words are used to describe the character's traits?

   _____

3. What method was used to make the character come alive? _____

It was well known that there was an old fox and his family living in the area. This fox was called "Scarface" because of a scar that reached from his eye all the way to the back of his ear. The winter before, I had met him and had had a sample of how smart and sly he could be.

4. Who are the characters in this passage? _____

5. What two words are used to describe Scarface's traits?

   _____

6. What method was used to make the character come alive? _____

And the living room would be full of church folks and relatives. There they sit, in chairs all around the living room, and the night is creeping up outside, but nobody knows it yet. You can see the darkness growing against the windowpanes and you hear the street noises every now and again . . . but it's real quiet in the room. . . . The silence, the darkness coming, and the darkness in the faces frighten the child. The darkness outside is what the old folks have been talking about. It's what they've come from. It's what they endure.

7. Who are the characters in this passage? _____

8. What are two words that could be used to describe the most important character?

   _____

9. What method was used to make the character come alive? _____

Read each paragraph and circle the answer for each question.

Someone outside the porch screen coughed. It was a messenger from one of the forest rangers. The ranger had written to say that a leopard had killed two oxen.

A short time later another message came. The leopard had killed again.

I wanted to hunt, and since my husband was away, no one could stop me. I sent a message to the forest ranger to say I was coming. Quickly I prepared for the adventure that lay ahead.

1. What words could be used to describe the woman?

   A cautious and fearful

   B lonely and sad

   C slow and thoughtful

   D fearless and eager

2. How do you know what she is like?

   F through narration and actions

   G through actions only

   H through dialogue

   J through dialogue and narration

As I walked along Tenth Street, I noticed a small store squeezed in between two huge brick buildings. The sign in red letters across the window said DANDY'S CANDY STORE. I sidestepped a kid whose dirty little fingers were busy tearing off the wrapper that hid his candy bar. I knew I had to have one.

I gave up the money to gently remove a wrapper and feast on the sweet chocolate. Then I rolled the candy wrapper between my palms into a tiny ball. I made a basketball from it and threw it toward an overflowing garbage can. It landed on the edge and fell to the sidewalk. I picked it up, partly because I didn't want to add to the mess on the pavement and partly because I didn't dig missing an easy basket.

3. How could the main character be described?

   A fearless and sly

   B lazy and afraid

   C relaxed and easygoing

   D foolish and thoughtless

4. How do you know what the character is like?

   F through narration and actions

   G through actions

   H through dialogue

   J through narration and dialogue

I have known a great number of charming animals, from mice to elephants, but I have never seen one to compare with Chumley for force and charm of personality. After knowing him for a while, you could not look upon him as an ape. You regarded him more as a courtly old man who had simply disguised himself. His manners were nearly perfect. He would eat slowly and politely. He pushed pieces of food he didn't want to the side of his plate. His only shortcoming in manners came at the end of the meal, for then he would grab hold of his empty mug and plate and hurl them as far as possible.

5. Who or what is the main character?

   A a zookeeper

   B an ape

   C a zoo patron

   D an animal trainer

6. How do you know what the character is like?

   F through actions

   G through dialogue

   H through narration

   J through narration and actions

 Introduce

Identifying Main Idea

The **main idea** is the most important idea in a passage. It is the point the writer is trying to make. Every passage has a main idea. Usually the other sentences supply supporting details.

The main idea may be stated in a sentence at the beginning of a passage, at the end, or in any other sentence in the passage. The main idea may be directly stated, or the main idea may be implied—not stated in any sentence.

To find the main idea, read the entire passage and ask yourself what it is about. Find a sentence that states that idea. If you do not find such a sentence, the main idea is probably implied.

Read each passage. Follow the directions.

A typhoon hit with full fury today on the coast of Japan. Heavy rain from the storm flooded the area. High waves carried many homes into the sea. People now fear that the heavy rains will cause mud slides in the central part of the country. The number of people killed by the storm may climb past the 200 mark by Saturday.

1. State the main idea in your own words. _____

_____

2. Underline the sentence that states the main idea.

The American author Jack London was once a pupil at the Cole Grammar School in Oakland, California. Each morning the class sang a song. When the teacher noticed that Jack wouldn't sing, she sent him to the principal. He returned to class with a note. It said he could be excused from singing if he would write an essay every morning.

3. The main idea in this passage is implied. Write the main idea.

_____

_____

Sledding is no longer just a winter sport. In fact, it is even becoming a popular sport in deserts. Desert sledders just head for a sand dune. They slide on plastic saucers, pieces of wood, or their own two feet. No matter which kind of sled is used, a great part of the fun is tipping over into the sand.

4. Underline the main idea if it is stated. Or, write the implied main idea if the main idea is not directly stated.

_____

B Practice

Read each passage. Then find the main idea and the best title for each one.

The sports car is popular for many reasons. The most important reason is that it can outperform other cars on narrow roads. This is why it was created in the first place. It is a safer vehicle on winding roads, too. The sports car is smaller, lighter, and lower than most cars. It can turn within a shorter radius. It weighs less, so the engine does not have to work as hard as the engine of a large car. The brakes do not have to work very hard either. Because of the low center of gravity, a sports car hugs the road at all speeds. It responds well when passing other cars. No wonder the sports car has always been a popular kind of car.

1. Underline the sentence that states the main idea of this passage.

2. Circle the best title for this passage.
   A   A Balanced Opinion
   B   A Close Look at Sports Cars
   C   Highways and Byways
   D   Safe Travel

When softball was first played, people thought of it as a simple batting and fielding game. Because of the large ball, the pitcher was looked upon as just another player. Softball pitchers soon learned that they could develop the speed needed to whiz the ball right past the batters. The pitcher became the key to a softball team's success. Babe Ruth learned this fact, much to his surprise. He was the greatest home-run hitter of his day. One evening, he was asked to play in a charity softball game at the old Madison Square Garden in New York City. The Babe hit several balls high up into the far reaches of the stands. Then a slim girl was introduced to the fans. To everyone's surprise, she was the next pitcher. Poor Babe Ruth struck out on three pitches he barely saw. The girl was a pitcher on a Western girls' team. She knew the art of softball pitching, and she knew the game.

3. Underline the sentence that states the main idea of this passage.

4. Circle the best title for this passage.
   F   Game for Charity in Madison Square Garden
   G   All's Well That Ends Well
   H   A Close Look at Baseball
   J   Softball Pitcher Strikes Out the Babe

The platypus has a bill like a duck's, and it lays eggs. Behind each ankle, the male platypus has sharp spurs that contain poison. It uses this poison to kill small animals, just as snakes do. Like the duck, the platypus has webbed feet. These make it a fine swimmer. In fact, it can swim as well as a fish. It has hair on its body, and the babies feed on their mother's milk. Worms and bugs are its favorite foods. When the first platypus was discovered, nobody could believe that it was real. The platypus seemed to be a little bit of everything.

5. Underline the sentence that states the main idea of this passage.

6. Circle the best title for this passage.
   A   Searching for Wild Animals
   B   Poisonous Animals
   C   The World's Strangest Animal
   D   Capturing the Platypus

Read each passage. Then circle the answer for each question.

The mudskipper is a remarkable fish that sometimes lives out of the water. It lives in the tropics in coastal areas along the Atlantic, Pacific, and Indian oceans, where the falling tides expose large mudflats in river mouths or mangrove swamps. Rather than retreating with the tide, mudskippers stay out on the mudflats, crawling or even hopping around on their well-developed front fins. Their eyes stick up on top of their heads. They hunt small crustaceans and other crawling creatures in the mud. As long as the air is not too hot and dry, they can remain out of water for several hours, until the tide returns, even though they have no lungs.

1. What is this passage about?
   A the walking fins of a mudskipper
   B ocean animals
   C mudflats inhabitants
   D the habits of a mudskipper

2. What is the implied main idea?
   F The mudskipper is an unusual fish that can live out of water for several hours.
   G Mudskippers are named for the way they can move around on the mud using their fins.
   H Some kinds of fish can do things that cannot usually be accomplished by fish.
   J Mudflats are the home of some unusual animals.

Most American think that denim is a fabric that originated in the United States. They get this idea because back in the late 1800s, at the time of the Old West, Levi Strauss designed sturdy denim pants—blue jeans—to be worn by miners, cowboys, and other people who did hard physical labor. But the truth is that the fabric from which jeans are made originated in France, in the city of Nîmes. The French word for *of* is *de*, so when people said that the fabric was "de Nîmes," they meant that it was "of the city of Nîmes" or, more simply, from Nîmes. The French pronunciation for *de Nîmes* sounds like denim.

3. What is this passage about?
   A the origin of denim
   B Levi Strauss and his famous pants
   C clothes of the Old West
   D French clothing design

4. What is the implied main idea?
   F Levi Strauss invented blue jeans in America.
   G Blue denim fabric was invented in the French city of Nîmes, from which it got its name.
   H The French contributions to the Old West were important.
   J The origins of some inventions are surprising.

Read each paragraph and circle the answer for each question.

(1) When building their homes, pioneers had to make use of whatever they could find at hand. (2) On the plains, where only a few trees grew, builders faced a serious challenge. (3) However, these people were not discouraged by the lack of wood. (4) The prairie settlers built their houses with the one thing that was common—sod. (5) The sod, or soil, containing grass and roots, was often six or more inches thick. (6) Packed by rain and hot sun, the sod became so hard that only a sharp plow could cut it. (7) The prairie settlers removed the sod in pieces about two feet long and one foot wide. (8) The big grassy chunks were stacked one on top of the other to form the walls of the sod houses.

1. What is this passage about?
    A   the sod houses of the prairie
    B   prairie life
    C   trees that thrive in prairie conditions
    D   growing sod

2. What is the best title for the passage?
    F   Building on the Prairie
    G   Sod Houses of Prairie Settlers
    H   Cutting Sod
    J   No Wood, No House

3. In what sentence is the main idea expressed?
    A   sentence 1
    B   sentence 4
    C   sentence 7
    D   sentence 8

Scientists have developed a simple method for finding out how much pollen is in the air. They take a meter-long glass slide, coat it with oil, and set it up in an open field. After it has been exposed to the air for several hours, the scientists take the slide and examine it with a microscope. When magnified, the pollen grains that have stuck to the oil can be counted, providing the "pollen count." The amount of pollen varies with different weather conditions; on a humid day there will be less, on a dry day, more.

4. What is this passage about?
    F   scientific experiments
    G   pollen counts
    H   the purpose of pollen
    J   weather conditions

5. What is the best title for the passage?
    A   The Effects of Pollen
    B   Studying Pollen
    C   How a Pollen Count Is Taken
    D   High Pollen Counts

6. In what sentence is the implied main idea best expressed?
    F   Scientists use on oil-coated glass slide to measure the amount of pollen in the air.
    G   Scientists have developed a method for studying pollen in the air.
    H   Pollen grains stick to the oil coating of a glass slide.
    J   Scientists magnify pollen to study it.

Read On   Read "Made for the Desert." Look for details that help support the main idea. Then answer the questions.

Finding the Main Idea

Each passage has a **topic**—what the passage is about—and a **main idea**—the most important idea. The main idea may be stated in a topic sentence, or the main idea may be implied, not directly stated in the passage. If the main idea is implied, the reader must use the supporting details to determine the implied main idea.

Read each passage. Answer the question, then follow the directions.

In 14th century Spain, men wore false beards that were dyed to match their clothes. Beards were quite fashionable among Spanish aristocrats, and some men changed their beards as often as they changed their clothes. They might wear a yellow or a crimson beard during the day and change into a long black beard to go to a formal party at night. The beards started to cause problems when some men used them as disguises. People wearing similar beards were often mistaken for one another, police arrested the wrong bearded men, and villains could escape trouble by changing their beards. Finally, King Philip IV outlawed the wearing of false beards.

1. Is the main idea stated or implied? _____

2. If the main idea is stated, underline the topic sentence. If the main idea is implied, write it.

_____

_____

People who read Chinese know more characters than anyone in the world. In this case, characters are the symbols that people use to write. We use characters in English, too. The 26 letters in our alphabet are characters. But characters in Chinese are much more difficult to learn than our letters. One reason is that there are around 40,000 of them. The average person, however, needs to know only a few thousand. Each character stands for a whole idea, thing, or sound. Also, the characters are much more detailed than our letters. This makes writing Chinese very difficult.

3. Is the main idea stated or implied? _____

4. If the main idea is stated, underline the topic sentence. If the main idea is implied, write it.

_____

_____

Read each passage. Then write the main idea, stated as a topic sentence, on the lines.

1.   At one time, you could buy tarts with the Queen of Hearts. You didn't have to be a joker in order to do so. Everyone was doing it. The first paper money in North America was playing cards. In 1685, the French colonial government was running low on money, so it started using cards from a standard playing deck as currency. These were signed by the governor and sent throughout French Canada. This system was only supposed to be used until the real money arrived from France. Yet it stayed around for the next hundred years because it was so popular.

_____

2.   Bread and other cereal grains should be an important part of people's diets. Cereal grains are grown all over the world and are by far the world's greatest crop each year. These grains are easily cultivated in the United States and produce a great amount per acre. They cost little to grow and can be easily stored. They should make up the largest single item in the average person's diet. Yet, this is often not the case. The U.S. Senate has determined that Americans need more whole grains in their diet. They now eat too much protein and fat. Many serious illnesses have been linked to high protein and fat diets. Grains need more preparation than "fast food," but they are better for us.

_____

3.   The piranha is a pretty fish, but don't let that fool you. Piranhas may be the most vicious fish known to humans. They do a lot more damage than sharks do. Piranhas are small fish, only 4 to 18 inches long, but their razor-sharp teeth make them deadly. They travel in schools of 1000 fish, and it takes them only minutes to turn a living human being into a skeleton. The people and animals that live near the piranhas' home in the Amazon River in South America know the perils of swimming when these creatures are near. As with sharks, the smell of blood is what causes these ferocious little fish to attack.

_____

4.   Its sweet taste isn't the only good thing about honey. Honey has been used as a medicine for centuries. The ancient Egyptians were almost honey addicts. Out of 900 of their medicines, 500 contained honey. Not all of the honey medications were meant to be tasted. In some cases, honey was used as an ointment. The Egyptians mixed honey with grease and rubbed it on small wounds and sores. Doctors today have found that this remedy does have a medical basis. Honey kills bacteria in wounds. This knowledge was helpful during wars when honey was used as a makeshift medicine.

_____

Apply

Read each passage. Then write the implied main idea of each one.

1. An exotic Indian tree is known to have a thousand or more separate trunks. The banyan tree, which is found in India, has this remarkable structure because of its tough, low-hanging branches. These branches grow down to touch the ground and then develop a set of roots of their own. Each branch becomes a new trunk. If there is enough space and soil, this process goes on until a single tree accumulates a thousand separate trunks, which are all part of the same plant. The largest banyan tree is on the island of Ceylon. It has 350 large trunks and more than 3000 small trunks.

_____

_____

_____

2. When the Pilgrims landed in New England, they knew little about the climate of their new home. October brought the first flurries of snow. Frost nipped the woods, and the chill of the air foretold the coming of winter. The Indians told the Pilgrims that summer would return before winter arrived, and they were right! In the last days of October, it grew warm once again. People have long referred to a short season of warm, pleasant weather that arrives after a frost but before the onset of winter as Indian summer. It usually occurs in the latter part of October or early in November.

_____

_____

_____

3. Every June, thousands of giant sea turtles come ashore in Florida and put on a great show for nature lovers. Thousands of people carrying cameras and binoculars line up on Jensen Beach to see the turtles lay their eggs. It's quite a spectacle. Some of these giant sea turtles weigh up to 500 pounds. They lumber ashore, dig nests in the moist sand with their heavy flippers, and deposit their eggs in the holes. Then the turtles cover the eggs with sand and pay no further attention to them. The warm sun helps the eggs hatch in about two months.

_____

_____

_____

4. Many people used to believe that if a fine tea is kept for too long, it will become stale and spoiled. Chinese tea drinkers have always disagreed. They have said that good black teas, like wine, improve with age. Some British tea merchants have begun to claim that common black teas are improved in flavor when they are aged for up to two years. More recently, people have discovered other sorts of teas that become more flavorful when they are allowed to age rather than being served fresh. It just goes to show that people's tastes can change.

_____

_____

_____

D ▶ Check Up

Read each paragraph and circle the answer for each question.

Bones can become as flexible as rubber or as brittle as china. Our bones are made from a mixture. One part is a fibrous protein called *collagen*. Collagen is soft and pliable. The other main ingredient in bones is *apatite*. This is a mineral made from tiny crystals of calcium phosphate. It is hard and breakable. If a bone's apatite is removed, leaving only the collagen, the bone becomes so rubbery that you could tie it in a knot. If the collagen is removed, the opposite happens. The bones become brittle.

1. What is the main idea?

   A   Bones are flexible and brittle.

   B   Bones contain a mineral called apatite.

   C   Bones are a mixture of substances.

   D   Bones are made of a mixture of apatite and collagen.

Do you know that a jellyfish is not a fish at all? It is an animal without a skeleton. Ninety percent of its body is composed of a jellylike substance. What the jellyfish lacks in bones, it makes up for in stomach. It is really just one big stomach cavity. It has no brain or blood vessels. The jellyfish has the ability to sting. It uses its sting to catch its dinner. One sting is usually enough to stun the jellyfish's prey. The jellyfish then reaches out with its tentacles and carries the helpless creature to the jellyfish's stomach.

2. What is the main idea?

   F   The jellyfish is a strange sea creature.

   G   The jellyfish isn't a fish at all.

   H   Ninety percent of a jellyfish's body is composed of a jellylike substance.

   J   A jellyfish is a boneless, stinging sea creature.

Many early people created myths and gods to explain nature. For example, lightning and thunder must have been very frightening experiences for ancient people. Early legends explain lightning as caused by various gods. Jupiter, for example, was the king of Roman gods and the god of thunder, lightning, and rain. Thor, a Norse god, was also a god of weather. Whenever they were displeased with people or with other gods, they would throw thunderbolts. These bolts were often accompanied by huge gusts of wind. Many early religions began with these myths, which were used to explain nature.

3. What is the main idea?

   A   Myths often developed into religions.

   B   The Romans created Jupiter as a weather god.

   C   Jupiter threw thunderbolts.

   D   Early people created myths to explain nature.

Read On   Read "A Man with a Vision." Look for the main idea of each paragraph or passage. Then answer the questions.

Comparing and Contrasting

To describe how two or more things are alike is to **compare** them. To describe how two or more things are different is to **contrast** them.

Words such as *alike, by comparison, similar to,* and *in the same way* often signal a comparison, while words such as *different, but, in contrast to, however,* or *although* often signal a contrast.

Read each passage. Then answer the questions.

Insects have a way of producing sound without using vocal chords. Beetles make whirring noises with their wings. Similarly, the hum of flies and bees is caused by the rapid vibration of their wings. Certain grasshoppers rub a hind leg against a vein in the forewing to "sing."

1. Is this passage a comparison, a contrast, or both? _____

2. What is a signal word or phrase that was used? _____

In a city, many people live in apartments. The apartments are as different as the people who live in them. Some apartments are small and compact, while others are large and spacious. Although an apartment is small, it may be bright and shiny, while a large apartment may be dark and drab.

4. Is this passage a comparison, a contrast, or both? _____

4. What two signal words or phrases were used? _____

Visitors to Chicago might enjoy visiting the Lincoln Park Zoo, the Adler Planetarium, and listening to jazz in the many small clubs around town. Like Chicago, New Orleans has jazz clubs, but visitors might also enjoy a ride on a paddleboat up and down the Mississippi River or a streetcar ride along St. Charles Avenue.

5. Is this passage a comparison, a contrast, or both? _____

6. What two signal words or phrases were used? _____

Read each passage then answer each question.

Many people have heard of killer bees, but how many of them have heard of killer ants? Killer ants, also called fire ants, are aggressive insects. Their sting can kill. Just like killer bees, the stings of fire ants can make people ill or even cause them to die. Neither insect is native to the United States. Both killer bees and fire ants came from other places.

1. What two things are being compared? _____

2. What are two ways in which they are alike?

   a. _____

   b. _____

People have been trying to cool and moisturize the air in their homes and workplaces since ancient times. The ancient Egyptians, Greeks, and Romans used wet mats to cool indoor air. They hung the mats over the doorways, and as wind blew through the mats, the evaporation of the water cooled the air inside. Leonardo da Vinci built the first mechanical fan in about 1500, using water power to turn the fan. The English developed a rotary fan in 1553 to ventilate coal mines. With the growth of industry, inventors worked on cooling systems for keeping workers comfortable and machinery in good running order. Today, people in many parts of the world depend on air conditioning to keep themselves cool.

3. What is being compared? _____

4. What are two ways that were compared?

   a. _____

   b. _____

Only three breeds of dogs have ever been known to achieve a weight of more than 220 pounds: the St. Bernard, the Old English Mastiff, and the Great Dane. All are very large, stocky dogs, and most of their weight is pure bone and muscle. These large dogs usually have a shorter life span than smaller breeds do. They usually live no more than 10 years, while terriers, for example, may live for as long as 15 years.

5. What is being compared? _____

6. What are two ways in which they are alike?

   a. _____

   b. _____

C Apply

Read each passage. Then answer each question.

Over short distances, the cheetah is the fastest animal in the world. But in spite of its great speed, a cheetah cannot catch an animal that has greater endurance. Because a cheetah cannot maintain its top speed for very long, it hunts by hiding close to a herd of animals and waiting until its prey comes close enough to attack. Its most common prey is the Thomson's gazelle, which can reach speeds of about 50 miles per hour. The gazelle possesses the ability to dodge, jump over uneven ground, and endure the chase. Cheetahs are most likely to catch the young or ill gazelles, playing the predator's usual role of removing from a herd animals that are weak or unhealthy.

1. What is being contrasted? _____

2. What are two ways in which they are different?

   a. _____

   _____

   b. _____

   _____

The English language contains hundreds of thousands of words, but many of them are old and seldom used anymore or are technical words. The average adult uses only about 3,000 words on a regular basis. That's twice as many as a five-year-old child knows when he or she enters school. By the time that child graduates from college, he or she knows 60,000 words but only uses 10 to 20 percent of them regularly. Writers use the most words on a daily basis. The average American journalist uses 6,000 different words to write newspaper articles. That's 4 percent of the total number of words in the language. Famous writers have used the most words of all. William Shakespeare, for instance, used 24,000 words in his plays and poetry. That's four times as many as a newspaper writer uses.

3. What is being contrasted? _____

4. What are two differences?

   a. _____

   _____

   b. _____

   _____

◆D Check Up

Read each passage. Then circle the answer that completes each statement.

The Indian elephant is the longest-lived land mammal, second only to human beings. It lives longer in captivity than it does in the wild, and the average life span for a captive Indian elephant is 60 years. By the time humans have lived 70 years or so, they've lost most of their teeth and have to wear dentures. When people have lost their permanent teeth, they don't get any more; _____, elephants, even as adults, have replacement teeth ready to grow in to take the place of those that wear out. But elephants do run out of replacement teeth, and if an elephant lived long enough, it could die of starvation if it wore down its last teeth.

1. This passage is an example of a

   A comparison

   B contrast

2. The best word or phrase for the blank in the passage is

   C similarly

   D by contrast

The woolly mammoths that lived during the Ice Age are _____ the modern-day elephants. Like the elephant, the woolly mammoth had a trunk and tusks. Similarly, the woolly mammoth was one of the largest land mammals of its time, just as the elephant is today.

3. This passage is an example of a

   F comparison

   G contrast

4. The best word or phrase for the blank in the passage is

   H similar to

   J different from

Travel by train and travel by air are quite abit _____. On the train, you watch the countryside pass by your window. In contrast, all you see from a plane are tiny patches of color and thin strips of water zooming by far below you. Trains make frequent stops while planes often don't stop until you reach your destination. Finally, though many people believe that train travel is relaxing, hardly anyone says the same about air travel. So, if you had a choice, which kind of travel would you use?

5. This passage is an example of a

   A comparison

   B contrast

6. The best word for the blank in the passage is

   C alike

   D different

A Introduce

Comparing and Contrasting

A **comparison** is a way of showing how things are alike. A **contrast** is a way of showing how things are different. Here are some words that signal comparisons and contrasts:

Comparisons		Contrasts	
like	just as	different	in contrast to
alike	compared to	but	contrasted with
similarity		however	

Read each passage. Then answer each question and complete each sentence.

There is a similarity between your body and a skyscraper. Neither could exist without a framework. Your framework is made of bones, while a skyscraper has a framework made of steel girders.

1. Is this passage an example of a comparison or a contrast? _____

2. The two things being compared or contrasted are a _____ and a _____.

3. The word _____ is a signal word.

4. In the last sentence, your bones are compared to _____.

Onions are grown all over the world, and every country seems to have its own special size, color, and flavor of onion. Onions grown in Spain are large and taste mild enough to be eaten raw. Bermuda onions are also large and mild but have a dark red or purple skin. North American onions are usually small and strong in flavor. But the citizens of Victoria, Texas, grow quite large, sweet onions. They call these onions Bohemian apples.

5. Is this passage an example of a comparison or a contrast? _____

6. The things being compared or contrasted are _____.

7. The signal word _____ is used more than once.

8. The _____, _____, and _____ of onions are

mentioned in the first sentence and are contrasted throughout the paragraph.

Read each passage. Then answer each question.

Almost all animals have voices. A few, like the giraffe, rarely use their voices. By contrast, other animals' voices are familiar to people—the songs of birds and the barking of dogs, for example. Scientists believe that birds' songs are used for mating calls and to claim their territories. Dogs growl when they are feeling angry or threatened and bark when they are feeling happy and excited.

1. Is this a comparison or a contrast? _____

2. What is compared or contrasted? _____

Camels and mules are both stubborn animals. Goods can be put on a camel only when it is kneeling. However, if the load is too heavy, it won't get up. Similarly, a mule becomes stubborn if its load is too heavy. Also, like a mule, a camel has a powerful kick, which it will use when annoyed.

3. Is this a comparison or a contrast? _____

4. What is compared or contrasted? _____

Gems rarely appear beautiful in their natural state. The sparkling features that most people identify with a diamond are hidden under a hard crust that must be removed. Similarly, the deep, velvety hue of the sapphire, the glowing, brilliant red of the ruby, and the soft, clear green of the emerald are all hidden from view in nature. These gems only display their true character after a lapidary, or gem cutter, has skillfully cut them into facets and polished them. The final beauty of a gem depends a great deal upon the success of this delicate operation.

5. Is this a comparison or a contrast? _____

6. What is compared or contrasted? _____

Many animals live short lives, reaching old age within a few years of their birth. For example, a mouse lives only about 3 years and an opposum only about 1 year. Birds, however, tend to live longer than most mammals do, and several species have been known to live for 40, 50, or even 60 years. Most longevity records are set by birds that are well cared for in zoos or in private homes. The longest-lived bird on record was a male Andean condor, which lived to be 72 in a Moscow zoo.

7. Is this a comparison or a contrast?

_____

8. What is compared or contrasted? _____

C Apply

Read each passage. Then circle the answer for each question.

A typical meal on the Western frontier might consist only of meat and biscuits. Although this was a simple meal compared to the banquets industry barons back East might eat, to busy ranchers and farmers, it was a feast.

1. What two things are contrasted?

   A   life in the West and East

   B   meals in the West and the East

   C   ranchers and farmers

   D   frontier and civilization

2. What signal word or phrase is used?

   F   typical

   G   simple

   H   compared to

   J   feast

Success or failure of ski resorts depends on the whims of nature. When there is little snowfall in an area, skiers have little desire to come to a resort. Other resorts with plenty of snow are more appealing choices. By contrast, when snowfalls are frequent and heavy, skiers crowd the resort and its slopes.

3. What two things are contrasted?

   A   success and failure

   B   the forces of nature

   C   resort operations

   D   effects of different amounts of snowfall

4. What signal word or phrase is used?

   F   whims

   G   when

   H   other

   J   by contrast

Buying a computer is not easy. Differences between computers, even of the same brand, are great. Some computers have more speed than others. Some have more RAM or more ROM or both than others. While CD-ROM drives have been common, DVD drives are fast becoming the norm. Perhaps the best advice to use when buying a computer is to buy one that best suits your needs and that you can afford.

5. What things are contrasted?

   A   RAM

   B   ROM

   C   DVD drives

   D   computers

6. What signal word or phrase is used?

   F   differences

   G   speed

   H   or both

   J   that best

Read each passage. Then write the answer to each question.

There have been many disasters involving ships. One of the most famous sinkings was the *Titanic*. Less well known was the sinking of the *Eastland* in Chicago. Both disasters involved the loss of many people's lives.

1. Is this passage an example of a comparison or a contrast?

   _____

2. What is compared or contrasted?

   _____

3. What signal word or phrase is used?

   _____

Many people from cultures throughout the world "talk with their hands" to some degree. People of the Middle East have over 200 distinct gestures. By contrast, the hands of most Westerners are almost silent.

4. Is this passage an example of a comparison or a contrast?

   _____

5. What is compared or contrasted?

   _____

6. What signal word or phrase is used?

   _____

In hot weather, what color of clothing should you wear? If you are outdoors in the sunlight, light-colored clothes are cooler. They reflect the sun's rays. Dark-colored clothing, on the other hand, absorbs the sun's light, making you feel warm.

7. Is this passage an example of a comparison or a contrast?

   _____

8. What is compared or contrasted?

   _____

9. What signal word or phrase is used?

   _____

Drawing Conclusions

What is a **conclusion?** A conclusion is a decision or opinion you make based on facts you have read or facts that have been inferred. Conclusions may also be based on your own experiences or knowledge.

More than one conclusion may be drawn from a fact or a given set of facts. Drawing a conclusion might be pictured as putting information together in the following way:

| Stated Facts | + | Implied Facts | + | Personal Experience and Knowledge | = | **Conclusion** |

Read the passage. Circle the answer that completes each statement.

At one time or another, most people suffer from hiccups. Few people realize that hiccups can be caused by different things. A hiccup, for example, can be caused by a full stomach or by tumors in the stomach. Or it can be brought on by drinking something hot or cold too quickly.

A hiccup is really the reverse of coughing. The diaphragm contracts and pulls air across the vocal cords. From there the air rushes suddenly into the lungs. This makes the "hic-uhp" sound.

Sometimes hiccups are so violent or long-lasting that medical help is necessary. In most cases, however, they stop quickly with no side effects.

1. From the fact that tumors in the stomach can cause hiccups, you can conclude that
   A a person who gets hiccups frequently should see a doctor
   B hiccups are harmless
   C standing on your head is sure to cure hiccups
   D doctors do not take hiccups seriously

2. From the first paragraph, you can conclude that hiccups occur most often
   F during moments of crisis
   G during meals
   H in times of excitement
   J in times of sadness

3. From the passage as a whole, you can conclude that hiccups usually signal
   A overworked lungs
   B a weak diaphragm
   C strained vocal cords
   D an irritated stomach

Read the paragraph. Write one conclusion that could be drawn based on each fact.

Severe storm warnings have been posted along the Gulf Coast. Hurricane Gillian is expected to strike land near Galveston. Forecasters expect the storm to strike before midnight. Electricity outages are likely. Water supplies may be contaminated by seawater. Extremely high tides are expected.

1. Severe storm warnings have been posted along the Gulf Coast.

   _____

   _____

2. The storm is expected to strike near Galveston.

   _____

   _____

3. The storm will strike before midnight.

   _____

   _____

4. Electricity outages are likely.

   _____

   _____

5. Water supplies may be contaminated.

   _____

   _____

6. Extremely high tides are expected.

   _____

   _____

C ▶ Apply

Read each passage. Complete each statement to show what conclusion can be drawn. Then circle the answer for each question.

The powerful Siberian husky is an Arctic sled dog. Many Inuit still use huskies to get from one place to another. Even though the snowmobile and the airplane have taken the husky's place in the larger villages, Inuit in most places still need their dog friends. The huskies can drag their master and a heavy load much farther than even a snowmobile can.

1. You can conclude that a husky is valuable because of its _____.

2. What helped you draw this conclusion?

    A stated facts

    B implied facts

    C personal experience and knowledge

Long ago, there were no yardsticks, rulers, or tape measures. When people first began to measure things, they used their own fingers or hands. They may have even used their arms or feet. "This is a three-finger spearhead," a person might have said, or "This fish is as long as my foot put down two times." When people measured things in that way, they were using fingers and feet just as we use inch and foot markings on a yardstick.

3. If people with different-sized feet measured the same thing in "feet," the results would be _____.

4. What helped you draw this conclusion?

    A stated facts

    B implied facts

    C personal experience and knowledge

The army has been interested in homing pigeons for many years. The idea of training pigeons to carry messages to planes in flight was worked out during World War I. In recent years, pigeons have been trained for night flying and for flying over water. It was learned that they would rather fly at night than fly over water. Many pigeons have been trained to carry messages from ships to shore. Some have even been trained to carry messages from shore to ships.

5. A conclusion that can be drawn from the first two sentences is that planes during World War I had no _____

6. What helped you draw this conclusion?

    A stated facts

    B implied facts

    C personal experience and knowledge

Read each passage. Then circle the answer that completes each statement.

Contrary to its name, catnapping isn't something that cats do. It's something that people do. A catnap is a short doze. People take catnaps when they don't have time to sleep properly. Thomas Edison was a great catnapper. He was an inventor, and his projects kept him up far into the night. He was often found sleeping on his workbench! Winston Churchill, too, was famous for dozing off during the working day.

1. You can conclude that people who take a lot of catnaps

    A are great and famous people

    B are healthier than people who sleep at night

    C are usually busy people who don't get enough sound sleep

    D never sleep at night

The quickest way to catch a cold is to shake hands with someone who has a cold or to touch something that a cold sufferer has touched. Research has proven that cold viruses are easily spread from person to person by people's hands. People with colds cover their mouths with their hands when they cough or sneeze. Because of this, doctors say that people with colds should wash their hands frequently and use personal bars of soap, towels, and wash cloths. Research has shown that paper tissues are better than cloth handkerchiefs because germs can live for several hours on cloth but are neutralized on tissues.

2. A reader can conclude that

    F cold germs live for several hours

    G fewer people would catch colds if cold sufferers washed their hands

    H cold germs are spread only by hands

    J cold germs live for many days

Sea level is an important benchmark for measuring landforms. A mountain is usually referred to as being so many feet above sea level. Death Valley, California, is below sea level. Not all sea levels are the same around the world, however. In Alaska, for instance, the level of the sea seems to be rising. In Galveston, Texas, sea level is falling. Generally, the sea level around the world is rising. This situation is due to the gradual melting of the polar ice caps. Of course, as the world's sea level rises, mountains around the world will be getting shorter.

3. A reader can conclude that sea level is

    A not a stable standard of measurement

    B rapidly changing everywhere

    C an ancient standard of measurement

    D never going to fall again

If you've ever read *Mutiny on the Bounty* or seen the film, then you know that the ship *Bounty* was on a mission to collect breadfruit. But what is breadfruit? Breadfruit is an important food for many people living on tropical islands in the Pacific. The fruit grows on a tall tree that is a member of the mulberry family. The fruit is covered with a rough-textured rind and is approximately the size and shape of a softball. The pulp is mealy; but when baked, it looks and feels like fresh bread.

4. It can be concluded that breadfruit

    F is the most widely eaten food on Pacific islands

    G tastes good

    H does not taste good

    J can grow only on tropical islands

Drawing Conclusions

A **conclusion** is a decision or opinion you form based on something you read or hear. Drawing a conclusion requires you to think about what is stated as well as using your own experiences. Drawing conclusions tests your ability to reason. Sometimes the author states the conclusion, but more often it must be inferred.

Read the passage. Circle the answer that completes each statement. Then underline the appropriate sentence.

In many places today, clams are not safe to eat because they come from dirty waters. However, during the first year of the Plymouth Colony, clams saved the Pilgrims.

Upon arriving, the Pilgrims dug big holes into the sides of hills to make "dugouts." They put up sod walls and roofs of tree bark. Each dugout would keep a family safe through the winter until the Pilgrims could build log cabins in the spring.

How would they feed themselves until then? The Pilgrims had muskets and crossbows, but not many of the people were good shots. They had fishing lines, but the hooks were too big for the fish in shallow Plymouth Bay. Only half of the 102 Pilgrims lived through that first winter. They all might have died if it had not been for the clam. The clam was a lifesaver in the truest sense of the word.

1. From the fact that most of the Pilgrims were not good shots, you can conclude that

    A crossbows are difficult to aim

    B religious convictions kept them from learning to shoot

    C the Pilgrims came well prepared

    D they would not be good at hunting game such as deer

2. From the fact that the Pilgrims brought large fish hooks with them, you can conclude that they

    F wanted to put the hooks to many uses

    G could not buy small hooks in England

    H had to take whatever was given to them

    J expected to catch large fish

3. From the passage as a whole and the fact that clams saved the Pilgrims, you can conclude that

    A clams are still popular in New England

    ⋋**B** digging clams was easier than hunting game

    C clams were not safe to eat in the Pilgrims' time

    D the Pilgrims' dugouts were nearly useless

4. Underline the sentence from which you can conclude that the dugouts were only temporary shelters.

B Practice

Read this paragraph. Then follow the directions.

Most earthquakes occur when rock slides along a crack, or "fault," in Earth's crust. The sliding causes vibrations. The vibrations move through the ground like waves though water. These "seismic waves" cause some areas to rise and others to fall. Cities are most affected when the waves make buildings collapse. Flexible buildings can move with these waves. They bend with them like trees bending in the wind. Rigid buildings do not bend. They are like stiff, dead branches. Buildings on solid rock tend to move with the rock. They "ride the waves" as if on a surfboard, and the rock absorbs some of the shock. Buildings on loose earth shake more violently.

Complete the conclusion that could be drawn from each fact.

1. **Fact:** Most earthquakes occur when rock slides along a "fault."

   Conclusion: The most dangerous place to be during an earthquake is

   _____

2. **Fact:** The vibrations move through the ground like waves through water.

   Conclusion: Shaking from an earthquake may be felt _____

   _____

3. **Fact:** Flexible buildings can bend with these waves, like trees bending in the wind.

   Conclusion: During an earthquake, flexible buildings are _____ likely

(less, more)

   to collapse.

4. **Fact:** Rigid buildings are like stiff, dead branches.

   Conclusion: During an earthquake, rigid buildings are _____ likely to

(less, more)

   collapse.

5. **Fact:** Buildings on solid rock move with the rock, which absorbs some of the shock.

   Conclusion: During an earthquake, buildings on rock are _____ likely

(less, more)

   to be damaged.

6. **Fact:** Buildings on loose earth shake more violently.

   Conclusion: During an earthquake, buildings on loose earth are _____

(less, more)

   likely to be damaged.

◆C Apply

Complete the conclusion that could be drawn from each passage.

Before and during the American Civil War, many slaves escaped to the North by the Underground Railroad. The "Railroad" was an escape route run by Northerners who believed that slavery should not exist. Their homes were the stations of the Railroad. They provided the fugitives with food and shelter and a safe hiding place until they could be sent on to the next station. Through this system, the slaves were fed and cared for until they reached Canada, where they could be free. It is estimated that the Railroad helped over 30,000 slaves escape to freedom.

1. The reader can conclude that Southern slave owners felt that the Underground Railroad

   should be _____.

Many people love tomatoes. They eat them in salads and sandwiches and all by themselves. But this wasn't always the case. Not so long ago, many people believed that tomatoes were poisonous. Then, finally, some brave people took a bite of one. The rest is history.

2. The reader can conclude that the first person to eat a tomato must have been

   _____.

By the 1500s, Lyons, France, had become the European center for silk weaving. During the early 1600s, King James I of England hoped to make England the center of the silk trade. Knowing that silkworms ate mulberry leaves, he had 10,000 mulberry trees planted at Buckingham Palace. However, there was one major flaw in the king's idea that prevented it from working. There are several types of mulberry trees. Red and black mulberry trees produce edible berries. But they don't attract silkworms. Silkworms only eat the leaves of white mulberry trees.

3. The reader can conclude that King James did not plant _____.

When people think about the sounds and feelings of summer, they often think about crickets. The sound of crickets on a summer's night can be very soothing. But some people like the cricket for another reason. They believe that it brings good luck. They will make an effort to keep crickets inside their homes to increase their good fortune. There are, however, other people who believe that crickets are bad luck and should be kept away at all costs. Thank goodness most people don't try to decide whether crickets are good luck or bad luck—they just enjoy their sound.

4. The reader can conclude that the only thing most people agree on, when it comes to

   crickets, is that _____.

Read each passage. Then circle the conclusion that completes each statement.

The kite was named after a bird called a kite. It was once a common bird of prey in England. The kite was noted for gliding easily on air currents with its wings spread. In the early 17th century, English children learned how to stretch thin paper over light wooden frames and sail the devices against the wind. The toys, which were invented in ancient China, resembled the English birds. The birds glided and sailed, and so did the kites, which is what the children called the new playthings.

1. It can be concluded that the Chinese

   A gave the name *kite* to the English

   B called kites by another name

   C also now use the name *kite*

   D were also familiar with the bird

People in England have been burning a material very much like dirt for centuries. The substance is known as *peat.* Peat is vegetable matter that has decayed in moist earth. Peat that is used as a heating fuel is dug out of the ground, shaped into bricks, and dried. Then it is burned like firewood. Peat is actually the first step in the creation of coal. Millions of years ago, as landmasses formed, vegetable deposits were buried at various depths in the earth. Deposits that were buried deeply were subject to great pressure and formed coal. Those that remained close to the surface formed peat.

2. A reader can conclude that

   F peat is actually dirt

   G if peat were put under great pressure for a long time, it would turn into coal

   H peat could be a solution to the energy crisis

   J peat burns better than wood

The nomads of the Sahara Desert are always traveling. Water is scarce in the desert, so the nomads must move from one freshwater supply to another. About the only places in which water can be found in the desert are oases. The Sahara, which is in northern Africa, is the size of the entire United States. But it has only ninety oases. The area around an oasis has trees and grasses on which the goats and camels of the nomads graze. Nomads camp at an oasis until their animals have eaten most of the plants. Then they pack up and travel to another water and food supply.

3. It can be concluded that a nomad's life

   A is very long

   B takes place within a small area

   C is one of wealth and riches

   D means traveling in order to survive

Some people call it the tiger of the sea. Most call it the barracuda. Fast and equipped with teeth as sharp as razors and powerful jaws, this fish is one of the most dangerous creatures on earth. It feeds mostly on smaller fish in the tropical Atlantic Ocean. But it does attack swimming humans. Naturalists have observed a shrewd hunting style in the barracuda. It waits unnoticed for its prey to swim by, then it suddenly pounces.

4. It can be concluded that the barracuda

   F is dangerous only to smaller fish

   G is especially dangerous because it uses surprise attack

   H should be easy to hunt

   J is not fierce as people think

 **Read On** Read "Chicago's Killer Heat Wave." Answer the questions, using information in the article to draw conclusions.

Recognizing Cause and Effect

A **cause** is an action or event that brings about other actions or events. An **effect** is the outcome of an action or event. Sometimes a cause-and-effect relationship is directly stated. Other times it is implied.

Certain words can signal cause-and-effect relationships. Some of them are *because, therefore, so, as a result, since, in order to,* and *if/then.*

cause   signal word   effect
↓   ↓   ↓
I dropped the paddle into the water, therefore, I had difficulty getting back to shore.

Underline the cause in each sentence once. Underline the effect twice.
Then circle the signal word or words.

1. Few people visited the antique shop and as a result, it went out of business.

2. The new ski-lift runs at the resort meant less crowding on the slopes, so more visitors flocked to the resort.

3. Mr. Davis turned the car around because he realized he had left an important report at home.

4. Maria has been considering a career in government, since reading the biography of Abraham Lincoln.

For each cause, write an effect.

5. Because I bit into the hot pizza, _____

_____

6. Since the movie we wanted to see was sold out, _____

_____

7. As a result of eating a spicy meal, George _____

_____

8. Because of the choppy sea, the little boat _____

_____

B ▶ Practice

Read each passage. Then follow the directions.

Most ducks have light, hollow bones. Light bones help ducks that feed on the surface of the water to stay afloat. Diving ducks have much heavier bones than surface-feeding ducks. Heavier bones allow them to stay underwater and chase fish.

1. Put an X in front of each cause found in the passage.

_____   **A**   Most ducks have light, hollow bones.

_____   **B**   Most ducks feed on the surface.

_____   **C**   Diving ducks have heavy bones.

_____   **D**   Diving ducks chase fish.

2. List two effects.

F _____

_____

G _____

_____

Most drakes (male ducks) are brightly colored so they attract attention during the mating season. However, at the end of the mating season, most drakes molt. That is, they lose their old feathers. Without their flight feathers, the drakes are unable to fly. They also lose their bright coloring and turn a drab brown.

3. Put an X in front of each cause found in the passage.

_____   **A**   Most drakes are brightly colored.

_____   **B**   Drakes molt at the end of mating season.

_____   **C**   Drakes can't fly.

_____   **D**   The drakes turn a drab brown when they molt.

4. List two effects.

F _____

_____

G _____

_____

C Apply

Read each passage. Then write one cause and one effect.

Insects seem to disappear during the winter. As a result, people thought that they died and were somehow reborn in the spring. Now we know that if you look closely, you can find insects in many stages of growth during the winter months.

1. **Cause:** _____

   Effect: _____

Except for a narrow strip around its shores, Greenland lies buried under a sheet of permanent ice. The ice is thousands of feet thick so that only the tops of the highest mountains extend above it. From this ice cap huge glaciers pour into the sea. Icebergs break from these glaciers and drift into the open seas. Sometimes they move thousands of miles to the south before they melt.

2. **Cause:** _____

   Effect: _____

Although the benefits of aspirin are great, some people cannot take aspirin at all. They get skin rashes or asthmalike reactions even from normal doses. A small number of people who suffer from asthma, hay fever, and other problems may also have a bad reaction to aspirin.

3. **Cause:** _____

   Effect: _____

Dolphins are the star performers in many aquariums. Dolphins can be trained to do many tricks for audiences. They can be taught to leap high in the air to grab a fish from their keeper's hand, to jump through a hoop, and to fetch a ball or stick that is thrown.

4. **Cause:** _____

   Effect: _____

Write *cause* or *effect* to identify the underlined part of each passage.

The people of ancient Egypt made mummies because <u>they believed that the dead lived on in the next world.</u> They wanted to preserve the bodies of the dead.

1. _____

Larry Fuentes of California wants to turn other people's trash into art. <u>Larry visits local garbage dumps on a regular basis, and he always keeps his eyes open for interesting junk shops, curbside trash, and litter.</u> He joins buttons, beads, and other found materials together to form sculptures, artworks that sell for thousands of dollars.

2. _____

If you started a company, what would you name it? George Eastman, an American inventor, was faced with that problem back in 1888. He had just invented a little camera, and he didn't know what to call it. Eastman wanted a short word that was easy to spell and to say. <u>Instead of using an existing word, he decided to make one up.</u> He liked the letter *K* because it was the first letter in his mother's maiden name. Thinking about it, he decided that two *K*s were better than one. He tried the *K*s with other letters until he finally came up with the name *Kodak*. Kodak has since become one of the most famous brand names in the world.

3. _____

Trees are an important natural resource. One man thought they were so important that they deserved a special day of honor. <u>J. Sterling Morton loved trees and was concerned about the speed at which they were disappearing.</u> In 1872, he helped convince the Nebraska Board of Agriculture to make April 10 a special day for planting trees. The day was named Arbor Day, because *arbor* is the Latin word for *tree*. The first Arbor Day was a resounding success.

4. _____

<u>Automobile windshields rarely shatter.</u> They may crack, but they do not splinter or fly apart. This is because all vehicles are equipped with laminated safety glass. This can be described as a glass sandwich made of two layers of plate glass with a sheet of plastic in between.

5. _____

All baseball bats are manufactured with the trademark running with the grain of the wood. When a player uses the bat, the trademark should be held up so that the ball hits the grainy side of the bat. If a batter is not careful to do this, <u>the bat may split and possibly strike someone.</u>

6. _____

Using Cause and Effect

Most stories and some nonfiction passages are built on cause-and-effect relationships. A **cause** may be an action or event that makes something else happen. The thing that happens is the **effect.** Causes and effects may be stated or implied. When reading a passage, ask these questions to find cause-and-effect relationships:

What happened?
Why did it happen?

Then look for signal words or phrases that state the connection between what happened and why. Here are some words or phrases to look for:

because	since
therefore	so
if/then	in order to

cause
↓
                    signal
                    word
                    ↓
We wanted to stay warm so we built a fire.
                              ↑
                          effect

Read each sentence. Then circle the answer with the most likely cause or effect.

1. Because they want to learn new skills, adults may
   A   visit a school
   B   take courses at night or on weekends
   C   go on an extended vacation
   D   hire a baby-sitter

2. The electrician turned off the power in order to
   F   test the electrical system
   G   check the light bulb
   H   be safe when making repairs
   J   replace a lamp

3. When running errands, Mrs. Evans always bought groceries last because she
   A   disliked grocery shopping
   B   needed to see how much money she had left
   C   wanted to do other things first
   D   didn't want the food to spoil

4. When a car is built, a suspension system is included because the designers want
   F   the car to have a safe, smooth ride
   G   a way to support the tires
   H   the car to brake smoothly
   J   passengers to be safe

B Practice

Read the passage. Then complete each statement by underlining a stated or an implied effect.

Like its relative the whale, the dolphin is not a fish but a mammal. A dolphin is warm-blooded and feeds its young on the mother's milk. It breathes air through a "blowhole" in the top of its head. The blowhole is the first part of the dolphin to break through the surface as the animal rises from the deep.

Dolphins have torpedo-shaped bodies and smooth, rubbery skin. A strong tail sends the dolphin cruising through the water at speeds up to 25 miles an hour. Dolphins often race with boats. They may come alongside and then rush forward to the bow. There they take their place in front of the boat. They may hold this spot for several minutes, as if daring the captain to race.

1. Dolphins are mammals; as a result, they
   A have compound eyes, like bees do
   B lay eggs, as birds do
   C have scales, like fish do
   D bear live young, as seals do

2. Dolphins are mammals and breathe through a blowhole; therefore, they
   F must come to the surface
   G can stay underwater all the time
   H also have gills
   J can cover greater distances than whales

3. Because a dolphin's body is smooth and graceful, the dolphin can
   A breathe air
   B hide behind rocks
   C swim fast
   D feed its young

4. Since a dolphin's tail is strong, a dolphin is
   F protected from its enemies
   G a natural hunter
   H able to break the surface of the water
   J a powerful swimmer

 **Apply**

Write a cause-and-effect sentence for each passage. Use one of the words or phrases in the box as a signal of the cause-and-effect relationship.

because	therefore	so
since	in order to	if/then

Abraham Lincoln had a tadpole. It wasn't the kind that has a slender tail and lives in ponds. Lincoln's lived in the White House. His "tadpole" was his young son, Thomas. One day when Thomas was a baby, Lincoln looked at him and chuckled. "He looks like a tadpole," Lincoln said. From that day on, the baby was called Tad—short for tadpole. He was known by that name to the nation.

1. _____

_____

People who like to dive often meet in Key West. From there, in pairs or in groups, they scatter to their favorite diving spots. The powdery sands of the Florida Keys are surrounded by clear waters. These waters are filled with marine life of many kinds and colors.

2. _____

_____

If you were told that a person had tears in his or her eyes, you would probably conclude that the person had been hurt or was feeling sad. Actually, people have tears in their eyes all the time. Eyes must be washed constantly, and the salty fluid that is made by the tear glands does the cleaning. The amount of fluid that is released is so small that it can drain into two small tubes that are located in the corners of the eyes and then down into the sinuses.

3. _____

_____

The fossil remains of clamshells from hundreds of millions of years ago provide clues about the ancient seas of the earth. Fossils are the preserved remains or traces of ancient plants or animals. Scientists study them closely, like detectives studying fingerprints, to learn the secrets they hold.

4. _____

_____

D ▸ Check Up

Read each statement. Then circle the answer with the cause or effect that completes each statement.

1. Because less than 50% of eligible voters vote in elections,

   A   more people should vote

   B   fewer elections are needed

   C   elections are not important events

   D   a minority, not a majority, of people decide outcomes

2. Information on the Internet comes from many different sources; therefore,

   F   people have fewer sources to choose from

   G   it presents many points of view

   H   Internet users get easily confused

   J   fewer sources are needed

3. If you see someone yawn, then you are likely to

   A   conclude the person is ill

   B   ask him or her to stop

   C   yawn also

   D   fall asleep

4. Many people buy videotapes rather than rent them because

   F   they hate the hassle of having to pick up and return tapes

   G   it is cheaper to own than rent

   H   they can view the video more than once

   J   they have more movies to choose from if they buy

5. Contact lenses are sometimes chosen over eyeglasses in order to

   A   make cleaning easier

   B   save money

   C   improve vision and appearance

   D   change eye shape

6. During a tornado, ordinary objects become deadly missiles; therefore,

   F   clothes sometimes end up in trees

   G   the wind must be calm

   H   the best shelter is underground

   J   everything should be brought inside before the storm

A ▶ Introduce

Summarizing and Paraphrasing

A **summary** is a brief retelling of the ideas in a passage. A summary is short.
A **paraphrase** is a restating of the information in a passage, sometimes on a sentence-by-sentence basis, in one's own words.

Read the passages. Based on the definitions above, label each numbered item either *summary* or *paraphrase*.

When people hear the words "endangered species," they usually think of mammals and birds. But this term doesn't always refer to mammals or birds. There are also insects that are endangered. The United States has a special office that keeps track of endangered species of all kinds. The people there have found that 26 different species of insects have become extinct. Presently there are 6 types of butterflies on the endangered list.

1. Many species of insects are endangered.

_____

2. Most people think "endangered species" refers to mammals and birds. But some insects are also endangered. A special office has discovered that 26 species of insects have become extinct. Today 6 types of butterflies are endangered.

_____

The male and female mosquito both feed on nectar and plant juices, but the female mosquito also gets its nourishment from the blood of people and animals. It has a sharp "beak" that it uses to prick a hole in human or animal skin. It then pokes a hollow tube, which is its mouth, into the hole and sucks out a drop or two of blood. When a person is pricked by a pin, the blood begins to clot immediately; but a liquid that the mosquito leaves under the skin prevents clotting. Most people are allergic to this liquid, and this is what causes the skin to swell and itch.

3. The male and female mosquitoes feed on nectar and plant juices, but only the female feeds on blood. Its sharp beak pricks a hole in the skin. A hollow tube in its mouth sucks out blood. It leaves a liquid that prevents clotting and causes the skin to swell and itch.

_____

4. Only female mosquitoes feed on blood from people and animals.

_____

Circle the answer with the best summary for each passage.

What color is the ocean three thousand feet down? It is pitch black. Although at its surface ocean water appears to be blue or green, in its depths there is no color. Color is the result of reflected light. On the ocean's surface, sunlight is reflected by the various living organisms in the water. They absorb some of the light and reflect the rest. If the water appears green, it is because green light is being reflected by the plants and minerals in the water. At three thousand feet, all the light has been absorbed by the organisms above. What keeps the fish from bumping into one another in the dark? Some sense objects by sonar, which is a way of bouncing sounds off objects. Other fish that live very deep in the ocean actually give off their own light.

1. **A** Light in the ocean is affected by the plants and animals in the water.
   B Some fish that live deep in the ocean give off their own light.
   C There is no color in the depths of the ocean because there is no light.
   D The ocean appears to have different colors.

A frog has no ribs and its chest does not expand and contract when it breathes. Unlike most air-breathing animals, the frog swallows air into its lungs rather than inhaling it. For this reason it is not necessary for the frog to hold its breath when it jumps into water. All the frog has to do is stop swallowing air. A frog can live for a long time without breathing because it gets part of its oxygen supply through its skin. In very cold weather, a frog will sink to the bottom of a pond and remain there for a long time. Its breathing movements stop and the blood circulating through its skin absorbs enough oxygen from the water to sustain life.

2. **F** In cold weather frogs stay on the bottom of ponds and absorb oxygen through their skins.
   G A frog has no ribs, and its chest does not move when it breathes.
   H The frog gets oxygen through its skin and by swallowing air.
   J Frogs can live for a long time without breathing.

Pigeons that are about to become mothers don't like to be alone. In fact, without company they couldn't lay their eggs. The pigeon's egg-laying system is very sensitive. It will function only under certain conditions. In order for the pigeon to lay her eggs, another pigeon must be around. It doesn't have to be the mother's mate. It can be either a male or a female pigeon. However, another pigeon must be present at the egg-laying. What's more, the mother must be able to see the other bird. Strange as it may seem, some pigeons have been known to lay eggs after seeing their own reflections.

3. **A** Soon-to-be pigeon mothers need a nest.
   B Pigeons have been known to lay eggs after seeing their own reflections.
   C The pigeon's egg-laying system is very sensitive.
   D In order for a pigeon to lay her eggs, she must be able to see another pigeon.

Apply

Write a summary and a paraphrase for the passage.

The Dead Sea is an inland lake located between Israel and Jordan. Lying 1296 feet below sea level, it is the lowest body of water on the earth's surface. The salt content of the water in the Dead Sea is about 270 percent as compared to the salt content of seawater, which is about 35 percent. Because the Dead Sea is an inland body of water, with no outlet, its salt content increases every year. A person can float on the surface of the water with ease. It is almost impossible to sink because salt water has a higher relative density (weight) than fresh water. Therefore, a person is actually lighter in salt water than in fresh water. The salt deposits in the water are so thick that they stick like glue to the skin, making them very difficult to remove. In fact, if one were to bathe in the Dead Sea, it would take days to remove the deposits of salt.

Summary

1. _____

_____

_____

_____

Paraphrase

2. _____

_____

_____

_____

_____

_____

_____

_____

_____

_____

Circle the answer with the best summary and the best paraphrase for each passage.

There are no furbearing animals of any kind on the land within the Antarctic Circle. There are no people who are native to this region either. The only human beings living at the South Pole are scientists who are studying the area. The penguin and a few other seabirds are about the only wildlife found in this icebound region. The only important mammalian life is the marine form. Some seals and a few whales live at the South Pole all year round. The absence of animals is one of the striking features of that continent.

1. **Summary**

   A The Antarctic is different from other areas on earth.

   B There is very little animal life in Antarctica.

2. **Paraphrase**

   C No furbearing animals live on the land within the Antarctic Circle. No native people live there either—only scientists. Penguins and other seabirds live there. The only mammals—seals and whales—live in the water. The absence of animals is a feature of the continent.

   D No animals live at the South Pole. The only humans are scientists. Some mammals—seals and whales—live in the water. No animals is one of the features of this area.

It is a common but false belief that porcupines shoot or throw their quills at an enemy when attacked. The truth is that the quills, or spines, stand upright when the animal is disturbed, just as a cat's fur does when the cat senses danger. The porcupine's quills are loosely attached to its body and tail and come out upon the slightest contact with other objects. When attacked, the porcupine thrashes about actively with its tail. If the tail comes into contact with anything, its quills are likely to become detached.

3. **Summary**

   F Porcupines do not "shoot" quills at their enemies.

   G Porcupines have an intriguing defense system.

4. **Paraphrase**

   H Porcupines do not shoot quills. When disturbed, the porcupine quills stand upright. The porcupine thrashes its tail. The quills come out.

   J It is a false belief that porcupines shoot their quills. The quills stand upright when the porcupine is in danger. The quills are loosely attached and come out easily. When attacked, the porcupine thrashes its tail. Quills may come out if the tail touches something.

Summarizing and Paraphrasing

A **summary** is a brief retelling of the ideas in a passage. When creating a summary, ask questions such as *Who?*, *What?*, *Where?*, and *When?* State the summary as briefly as possible while including the key points.

A **paraphrase** is a restating of the information in a passage. In a paraphrase you restate the sentences in the passage in your own words.

Read the passage. Label each numbered item as either a *summary* or a *paraphrase*. Then circle the answer with the best summary and the best paraphrase for the passage.

The frogfish, which lives near the bottom of the ocean, uses the tentacles that grow out of its head to catch other fish. On the end of each tentacle is a tiny hook that looks like the curved fish hooks that are used on fishing lines. The frogfish lies in wait with its tentacles floating in the water. Small fish mistake the hooks for worms, swim close to the tentacles, and are captured and immediately gobbled up by the crafty frogfish.

1. The frogfish uses its tentacles to catch the fish that it eats.

   _____

2. The frogfish eats small fish it has captured.

   _____

3. The frogfish catches other fish. Tiny hooks on tentacles float in the water. Small fish are captured and eaten up. This system of fishing is unusual for a fish to use on other fish.

   _____

4. The frogfish has an unusual way of capturing its prey.

   _____

5. The frogfish uses tentacles that grow out of its head to catch fish. Each tentacle ends in a tiny hook, like a fish hook. The frogfish waits with its tentacles floating in the water. Small fish, thinking the hooks are worms, swim close, get captured, and are gobbled up.

   _____

Circle the answer with the best summary for each passage.

A man named Lord Balfour believed that if you stared at the back of a person's head you could make him or her turn around. He thought this was a most amazing thing. The only amazing thing about it, however, was that it was not true. Because of widespread curiosity about this phenomenon, numerous experiments on the subject were conducted. All ended in failure. In one test at Stanford University, 12 people all stared at someone at the same time. The person being stared at did not know it and didn't turn around. So much for this amazing phenomenon.

1. A Some people believed that staring at the back of a person's head would make him or her turn around.

   B Tests done at Stanford University to test the theory that staring at someone from behind would make him or her turn around proved that the theory was false.

   C People sometimes believe things that have no element of truth.

   D Experiments are the best way to prove theories.

Many people think that the Caesar salad was named after the ancient Roman Emperor Julius Caesar. The truth is that the salad made its appearance fairly recently. It was named after Caesar Cardini. Cardini was an innkeeper in Mexico. One day, over 50 years ago, he ran out of food to serve. It was July 4, and there were a lot of hungry mouths to feed. The inn's ice chest was practically bare. All that remained were some romaine lettuce, some eggs, and some lemons. Cardini managed to find a bit of stale bread, romano cheese, and some spices. That's all Caesar needed to make his famous salad.

2. F Necessity is sometimes the mother of invention.

   G The first Caesar salad was made by Caesar Cardini over 50 years ago.

   H The Caesar salad is a recent invention.

   J The Caesar salad was invented in Mexico.

A time capsule is not a pill. It is a container full of memories and history. Time capsules are made to communicate with people of the future. They are containers that are filled with souvenirs and buried under famous places or sealed into the corners of buildings. One capsule was buried in 1940 under the site of the New York World's Fair. It was long and thin, like a torpedo, and made of metal. The capsule contains a history of the world, copies of some famous paintings, a Bible, a toothbrush, and even some baseball cards. Time capsules are created in the hope that people in the distant future will discover them and learn how we lived, for our present will be their past.

3. A Time capsules are a fairly recent communication device.

   B Time capsules are made to tell people what our way of life is like.

   C Time capsules preserve the past for future generations.

   D Time capsules contain souvenirs.

Write a paraphrase of the passage.

It you wanted to build yourself a house, you would have a tough choice when it came to building materials. Houses can be built out of many different materials. Some are molded out of concrete. Others have siding that's made of aluminum. Still others are built from extra strong plastic.

The materials for houses in the past were much simpler. Old English houses and castles were built out of stone. In pioneer America, the most popular building material was wood. Abraham Lincoln's famous boyhood home was a log cabin. But do you know what the oldest building material is? It's brick. As far back as ancient Egypt, people used these blocks of hardened clay.

_____

_____

_____

_____

_____

_____

_____

_____

_____

_____

_____

_____

_____

_____

_____

Write a summary and a paraphrase of the passage.

There's a good reason why a dog pants heavily when it has overexercised itself. A dog can't cool itself off by sweating, the way people do, because dogs don't have as many sweat glands. A dog must rid itself of excess heat by breathing. Its tongue will hang from its mouth while it pants to provide a large surface from which the extra heat in its body can evaporate. Although a dog is able to lose most of its excess heat by panting, it has sweat glands on its nose and paw pads. These extra sweat glands also help the dog rid itself of extra heat.

1. **Summary**

_____

_____

_____

_____

_____

2. **Paraphrase**

_____

_____

_____

_____

_____

_____

_____

_____

_____

_____

Using Supporting Evidence

Most passages have at least one **main idea.** The main idea is the most important idea in the passage. The main idea may be stated in the passage, or you may have to infer what it is.

The phrases or sentences that tell about the main idea are **supporting evidence.** Not all sentences in a passage provide supporting evidence.

In this passage, the main idea appears in boldfaced type. The supporting evidence is underlined.

In nature, there are patterns that repeat. One example is the seasons of the year. Another example is the phases of the moon. Can you name some others?

Circle the main idea in the following passages. Then underline the supporting evidence.

1. America has many outstanding land features. Dense forests run along our northern border. Dry deserts cover the southwest. One of the longest rivers in the world divides one-third of our country from the rest. In addition, there are mountains in the East and West.

2. Born in 1867 in Lake Pepin, Wisconsin, Laura Ingalls Wilder, along with her family, lived in a log cabin. It was located at the edge of a large woods. Later they moved to Kansas, Minnesota, and the Dakota Territory. Laura Ingalls Wilder spent her early life in the Middle West.

3. Clocks have not always ticked. At one time, they dripped, and at another time they were totally silent. The first clock is believed to have been a pole stuck in the ground. Its shadow moved as the sun traveled across the sky. The Babylonians used this shadow method to tell time, and the ancient Egyptians made the first sundials based on the same idea. The Egyptians also used water clocks, which consisted of a basin of water with a small hole in the bottom.

Circle the answer to each question. Follow each direction.

In 1624 Captain John Smith called poison ivy the "poysoned weed." Poison ivy is a weed that contains a poisonous oil. Experiments have shown just how strong the oil is. In one study, a glove was brushed against a poison ivy plant and put aside for ten months. It was then washed for ten minutes in hot water and strong soap and pressed with a hot iron. A woman handled the glove. The next day she had poison ivy on her hands. People used to think the plant gave off fumes that could affect people. We now know that this idea is false. But if the plant is burned, poison ivy can be carried through the air. The sap clings to the ashes. Animals, too, can carry the oil from poison ivy on their fur.

1. What is the paragraph mainly about?

   A the treatment of poison ivy

   B poison ivy's poison and how it spread

   C the shape of poison ivy leaves

   D poison ivy compared with poison oak

2. Underline the sentence that best states the main idea.

3. Which sentences are examples of supporting evidence?

   F All the sentences

   G None of the sentences

   H All but the main idea sentence

   J All but the first sentence

Fire is one of the oldest ways of measuring the passage of time. Long ago in England, candles were made with bands of black and white. Each band was made wide enough to burn in half an hour. The Chinese and Japanese burned ropes to tell time. Knots were tied in a rope at equal distances apart. When the rope was hung, the burning of each knot showed that an hour had passed. People in Holland and Germany told time by looking at the hour marks on the oil wells of lamp clocks. As the flame burned, the level of the oil in the well went down. Thus, the height of the oil in the well told the time.

4. Underline the sentence that states the main idea.

5. Which sentence supports the main idea?

   A The Chinese and Japanese burned ropes to tell time.

   B England is the clock capital of the world.

   C The pocket watch was most popular during the early 1900s.

   D Water clocks were used by the people of ancient Egypt.

6. How is the supporting evidence related to the main idea?

   F The supporting evidence defines what a clock is.

   G All the supporting evidence compares clocks to timepieces.

   H The supporting sentences give examples of fire clocks.

   J They all state reasons why the early clocks were not accurate.

C Apply

For each main idea, give three examples of supporting evidence that might appear in a passage along with that main idea.

Birds build their nests in unusual places.

1. _____

_____

2. _____

_____

3. _____

_____

Washington, D.C., has many places of historical interest.

4. _____

_____

5. _____

_____

6. _____

_____

The most crucial factor in making good pizza is the ingredients.

7. _____

_____

8. _____

_____

9. _____

_____

D ▶ Check Up

Read the paragraphs. Then circle the answer for each question.

(1) Most candidates who are running for political office cast a vote for themselves on election day. (2) This is true for any office, from town council representative to president of the United States. (3) In fact, the only U.S. president who did not vote for himself was Zachary Taylor, the 12th president. (4) It wasn't that Taylor didn't have faith in himself or didn't want the job. (5) He simply didn't qualify to vote because he was not a resident of any one state in the country. (6) Because Taylor was a professional soldier, he had to move around a lot. (7) Because he did not have a permanent home, he couldn't vote.

1. What is the main idea?

   A Certain requirements have to be met in order for a person to qualify to vote in an election.

   B Zachary Taylor was the only American president who didn't vote for himself.

   C Zachary Taylor couldn't vote in his own presidential election because he couldn't find the polls.

   D Zachary Taylor did not believe he was the best candidate.

2. Which sentence provides the most important supporting evidence related to the main idea?

   F sentence 3

   G sentence 5

   H sentence 6

   J sentence 4

(1) Vitamin E can be found in a number of foods. (2) Vegetable oils, margarine, eggs, and liver are especially good sources. (3) This vitamin plays a role in the prevention of certain blood disorders. (4) It helps prevent cell membranes from being destroyed by substances that build up around the membranes and cause them to break down. (5) These substances tend to increase in quantity as a person grows older. (6) For this reason, vitamin E has been suggested as a remedy for the effects of aging. (7) However, doctors and researchers are still studying the vitamin to find out if there is any real connection.

3. What is the main idea?

   A Vitamin E may help reverse the aging process.

   B Liver and eggs are foods high in vitamin E.

   C Vitamin E, which is found in certain foods, prevents some blood disorders and the destruction of cell membranes.

   D The healthiest remedies can often be found in natural substances.

4. Which two sentences provide the most important supporting evidence related to the main idea?

   F sentences 1 and 2

   G sentences 3 and 4

   H sentences 2 and 7

   J sentences 4 and 5

Read On   Read "A One-Sided War." Use skills developed in Lessons 9–13 to answer the questions.

Characters

Words and actions reveal a character's traits and motives.

Main Idea

The main idea is the most important idea in a paragraph. Sometimes it is stated directly. Sometimes you have to read all the sentences and think about the central idea they give you.

Compare/Contrast

Comparisons show how people and things are alike and contrasts show how people and things are different.

Drawing Conclusions

Conclusions are decisions you make using facts and experiences. Your conclusions are based on things that are stated directly, things that are implied, and things that you already know.

Cause and Effect

Authors use cause and effect to explain how one event causes another. Why something happens is the cause. What happens is the effect.

Summarizing and Paraphrasing

In a summary, you use your own words to give the main ideas of a passage. You *do not* include a lot of detail.

In a paraphrase, you restate the sentences in a passage in your own words. You *do include* details.

Supporting Evidence

Writers use supporting evidence to support statements in their writing. Supporting evidence can be facts, statistics, examples, or reasons.

Assessment

Read the paragraphs and circle the answer for each question.

You may know how to identify some trees by their leaves. But did you know that a tree can also be identified by its bark? Each type of tree has its own special bark. The barks of various trees differ in thickness and color. Some trees, such as the birch, have smooth, papery layers of bark. As the tree grows, one layer of bark peels off and another appears. Other trees, such as redwood and oak, have one rough, thick layer of bark that cracks and breaks as the tree trunk grows larger. The colors of bark range from the white of some birch trees to the dark brown of the walnut tree. Whatever its thickness or color, bark protects a tree against bad weather, insects, and even forest fires.

1. What is the best paraphrase of this paragraph?

    A Trees have different kinds of bark. Some bark is smooth. Some bark is rough. Bark is different colors.

    B You can identify a tree more easily by looking at its bark than at its leaves. Some bark looks like paper and peels off one layer at a time. Some bark breaks off as the trunk gets larger. Bark protects trees.

    C Some trees have smooth bark that comes off in layers like a birch tree. Oak trees have rough dark brown bark. Bark protects the trees from damage.

    D Trees can be identified by both their leaves and their bark. Different kinds of trees have different kinds of barks. The bark is different in thickness and color depending on the type of tree. All bark protects trees.

2. From this paragraph you can conclude that bark serves as a tree's

    F color

    G sound

    H armor

    J food supply

For those who are impressed by sheer size, Mount Rushmore is *the* sight to see. The faces of four American presidents are carved into the face of a mountain that is 5735 feet high. The granite sculpture is located in the Black Hills of South Dakota. American sculptor Gutzon Borglum designed the memorial and supervised most of its work. The four men it honors are George Washington, Thomas Jefferson, Abraham Lincoln, and Theodore Roosevelt. Each face measures 60 feet from chin to forehead. That's twice the height of the Great Sphinx in Egypt.

3. What is the main idea of this paragraph?

   A Mount Rushmore is a huge carving in the Black Hills that honors four American presidents.

   B Mount Rushmore is a bigger sculpture than the Great Sphinx.

   C The size of Mount Rushmore is what makes it great.

   D Gutzon Borglum is a sculptor with great vision and talent.

4. Which sentence does *not* support the idea that Mount Rushmore is *the* sight to see?

   F The faces of four American presidents are carved into the face of the mountain, which is 5735 feet high.

   G American sculptor Gutzon Borglum designed the memorial and supervised most of its work.

   H Each face measures 60 feet from chin to forehead.

   J That's twice the height of the Great Sphinx in Egypt.

Like cats, lizards normally dislike water. They drink water, of course, but they never go swimming. They don't even play near water. But one type of lizard, the basilisk, is a little more daring. Basilisks are found in Central and South America. In most ways they look like other lizards. Their bodies are long, often about two feet, and thin. Their legs are long and thin, too. But at the end of their thin legs, basilisks have broad feet that resemble fins. When a basilisk is fleeing from an enemy, it may hop right in the water. It doesn't swim away from the foe, however. In fact, it hardly gets wet. The basilisk's special feet enable it to walk on the water's surface.

5. The first sentence compares lizards to

   A other lizards

   B reptiles

   C cats

   D fish

6. A basilisk hardly gets wet when it is in the water because

   F its special feet enable it to walk on the water's surface

   G it is daring

   H it has a long thin body and legs

   J it is like a cat

Gail sat on the edge of the field watching her teammates run up and down the soccer field. They were exhausted and time was running out. They were two goals behind. "I know we can beat the other team," murmured Gail, clenching her hands. She looked at the coach, silently begging to be put into the game. Coach Ruiz sighed and said, "Do whatever you can, Gail, but it doesn't look good." Gail ran onto the field and yelled encouragement to her team. She cornered the ball and raced down the field before her opponents had time to catch their breaths. In an instant, she narrowed the gap to one goal. Gail had breathed new life into her dragging team. She gathered the girls into a huddle and said, "Just one more. Let's do it!"

7. What can you conclude about Gail's character?

   A She is lazy.

   B She is competitive.

   C She is slow.

   D She is inefficient.

8. Which word describes Gail's actions toward her teammates?

   F critical

   G depressing

   H encouraging

   J matter-of-fact

Bottles and glasses are like soap bubbles that last. The ingredients that make glass start off as a melted, syrupy mixture. A ball of that mixture is attached to the end of an iron glass-blowing pipe. The blower then puffs gently into the other end of the pipe. The glass inflates just as a soap bubble does. Expert glassblowers can mold the bubble into any shape they want it to be. As long as the glass is being heated, it can be shaped and reshaped. When the glassblower is satisfied, the glass is set aside to cool and harden.

9. In what way is glass different from a soap bubble?

   A Glass is clear.

   B Glass will not pop.

   C Glass is not blown.

   D Glass is formed from a liquid.

10. The first sentence is an example of

   F a comparison

   G an opinion

   H a cause

   J an effect

Extending Meaning

Sensory Language

Authors use sensory language to evoke meanings, associations, and memories. Sensory language appeals to the five senses. Write three words that appeal to each of the senses. Then choose one word from each group and use it in a sentence.

Sight: _____ _____ _____

_____

_____

Sound: _____ _____ _____

_____

_____

Smell: _____ _____ _____

_____

_____

Taste: _____ _____ _____

_____

_____

Touch: _____ _____ _____

_____

_____

Connotations

Many words have connotations, or meanings that go beyond their exact dictionary definitions. A word's connotations may include feelings, images, and memories the word suggests. On the lines under each word, write three connotations.

picnic

1. _____

2. _____

3. _____

dog

4. _____

5. _____

6. _____

concert

7. _____

8. _____

9. _____

car

10. _____

11. _____

12. _____

winter

13. _____

14. _____

15. _____

school

16. _____

17. _____

18. _____

Many connotations are based on positive or negative feelings. Write words with positive or negative connotations to complete the chart.

Positive	Negative
scent	
	babble
cozy	
	lazy
cautious	

Predicting Outcomes

What does it mean to **predict an outcome?** It means to make a logical guess about what will happen next based on the information you have. For example, suppose you read about a person putting on a bathing suit, smearing on sunscreen, and then picking up a towel. A prediction—a logical guess based on the information you have been given—would be that the next thing the person will do is go swimming.

Write your prediction.

Zachary Taylor preferred to save his money rather than spend it on his mail. Postage stamps had not yet become common in the mid-1800s, and most mail was delivered postage-due. Because Taylor was a well-known hero of the Mexican War, he received lots of mail from people he didn't know. Rather than pay the postage for all that mail, Taylor simply refused to accept it. In June of 1848 the Whig Party sends Taylor a letter informing him that he has been chosen as the Whig candidate for the United States presidency. What do you think will happen?

1. _____

_____

Humans may be the most intelligent form of life on this planet, but there are some things only animals can do. When it comes to predicting earthquakes, for instance, few scientists can top animals. Though the average person might have little idea that an earthquake is about to take place, the creatures of the wild can tell when such a natural disaster is approaching. Chickens in a barnyard, for example, will scurry about in a frenzy. Dogs will howl, and horses and oxen will become extremely restless. Many animals enter a state of nervous anticipation before an earthquake. What can you expect if you see animals making a big stir?

2. _____

_____

Ellen is a talented composer who wants to go to music school. She has tried hard all her life to be the best in everything she does. One of her teachers says that she will never be accepted to a music school because she isn't good enough. What will Ellen do next?

3. _____

_____

B ► Practice

Predict the outcome. Circle the statement that best predicts what will happen next.

Icebergs, unlike sea ice, are composed of fresh water, not sea water. The ice in the Antarctic bergs was created by the buildup of snow and its compression into ice during millions of years over the Antarctic continent. The ice flows toward the continent's edge. At the coast, it forms ice shelves about 240 meters thick that are continually breaking off and forming icebergs. Some of these icebergs are large enough to provide fresh water to a city the size of Washington, D.C., for thousands of years. The water in this ice is extremely pure, having the purity of distilled water. This frozen water merely drifts northward and eventually melts uselessly into the sea. What will a thirsty world do?

1. **A** People will decide to let icebergs melt to keep the ocean at normal levels.

   B Scientists will look for ways to use icebergs for fresh water.

   C People will blow icebergs up.

   D People will decide that icebergs have no practical value.

Many tales and legends have been told and written about the red fox, who is often portrayed as sly and clever. One of these, called "The Fox and the Fleas," tells about a fox with a flea problem. Hoping to rid himself of fleas, the fox decides to submerge in water and "drown" them off. So holding a forked branch in his mouth, he slowly sinks beneath the surface of a lake. As the water laps over his fur, the fleas abandon their place in his fur and make for the forked branch, the only dry spot around. What happens next?

2. **F** The fox swims to shore, clutching the branch.

   G The fleas then swim to shore.

   H The fox then releases the branch, and the fleas float away.

   J The fox has a change of heart and helps the fleas to shore.

Most people think that mice have an irresistible craving for cheese. In fact, most rodents are herbivores, or plant eaters, by nature. But people have influenced the eating habits of some mice. House mice will eat almost anything that people eat, such as grain, meat, and vegetables; they'll also chew up glue, leather, paste, and soap. A house mouse that finds itself outdoors may eat insects and the leaves, seeds, roots, and stems of plants. Mice are always looking for food, but they actually need to eat very little in order to survive. If a mouse gets into your house, what will it do?

3. **A** The mouse will ignore food and eat only glue and soap.

   B The mouse will eat any food you leave out.

   C The mouse will try to get outside.

   D The mouse will eat itself to death.

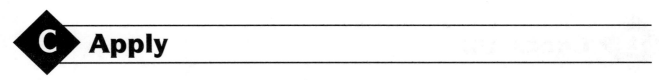

C Apply

Predict the outcome. Write what you think will happen next.

Though few people are aware of it, a 16-year-old girl made a more successful ride than Paul Revere and with the same purpose in mind. On April 27, 1777, the captain of the Connecticut militia received word that British troops had crossed Long Island Sound and burned down the town of Danbury. All the farmers had to be called out to fight. The captain's daughter, Sybil Ludington, volunteered to ride to each farmhouse to spread the word. And spread the word she did. Sybil rode over 40 miles through pitch darkness, banging on every door she passed to shout, "The British are coming!" What do you think the farmers who heard her warning did next?

1. _____

_____

_____

Good advertisements can help volunteer organizations get support from the public. An example is the Red Cross. During the first World War, the American Red Cross had a poster that came to symbolize the spirit and the purpose of the organization. The poster showed an older woman lovingly cradling a wounded soldier. The woman represented the Red Cross, which is devoted to the care of the sick and injured all over the world. The poster became so popular that it was used in Great Britain as well. What do you think people did after they saw the poster?

2. _____

_____

_____

A superstitious California woman spent four decades adding rooms to her house. By the time she died, Sarah Winchester's house was eight stories high and had over 160 rooms. Ms. Winchester believed that she would die if she stopped adding rooms to her house, so she constantly built new rooms. She added rooms of greatly varying sizes; some were palatial ballrooms, while others were tiny nooks barely one foot wide. Her house had miles of corridors and staircases that led nowhere. She had nine kitchens, thousands of windows, and countless doors. How long do you think Ms. Winchester continued to add to the rooms in her house?

3. _____

_____

_____

D Check Up

Predict the outcomes. Circle the answer that gives the most logical prediction.

The waterworks of ancient Rome were so advanced that they make even some of today's systems seem crude by comparison. The Romans had three water-supply systems. One system brought water to homes through pipes. Another system fed the public baths.

1. What do you think the third water-supply system was used for?

    A for the beautiful pools and fountains in the city

    B for shipping things up the Tiber River

    C for bringing water into homes

    D for transporting soldiers on rivers

A famous nature photographer was taking pictures in the rain forest near a precarious slope. Trying to get a better view of a pair of monkeys in a tree, she stretched out, balancing on her left leg while reaching forward with her right. Suddenly, she began to slip on the damp earth and wet leaves. Luckily, as she began to slide, she was able to reach out with a free hand.

2. How will the nature photographer be saved?

    F She will be able to grab a monkey who will pull her up.

    G She will grab hold of a camera bag.

    H She will regain her balance.

    J She will grab a mass of dangling tree roots.

Dan Hager was eager to enter the essay contest held by the local newspaper. The deadline was the next morning at ten o'clock. He was just revising his first draft when his friend, Barney, called with tickets to the local minor league baseball team's play-off game. Dan is not much of a baseball fan.

3. What will Dan do?

    A He will go to the game and forget the essay.

    B He will stay home and finish the essay.

    C He will write at the game.

    D He will write all night after going to the game.

For years, Liz has been interested in ancient Egypt. She has read all she can about the culture of ancient Egypt and has seen movies about the country. She has learned the language and has visited museums with Egyptian collections. Liz inherits five thousand dollars.

4. What will Liz do next?

    F Liz buys a movie about Egypt.

    G Liz travels to Egypt.

    H Liz invests the money.

    J Liz gives all the money away.

Read On As you read "The Threat of Mount Rainier," predict outcomes to help answer the questions.

Predicting Outcomes

When **predicting outcomes,** use what you know to guess what will come next. Look for these kinds of clues:

- clues that suggest what will happen next in a sequence of events
- clues that state causes and suggest possible effects
- clues that suggest how a person will behave in a given situation

Predict the outcomes. Complete the sentence. Write what you think will happen next.

As president of the United States, George Washington posed for a young artist named Joseph Wright. Wright intended to make a bust of the president wearing a solemn expression. The artist first placed Washington flat on his back on a cot. He then oiled his face and began applying the plaster for the mold. Just as the last of the plaster had been applied, first lady Martha Washington entered the room. When she saw her husband stretched out on the cot with his face covered in plaster, she gave a little cry of surprise. This amused the president, and he smiled. As a result,

1. _____

_____

_____

Judging from its sales, Worcestershire sauce is a favorite flavoring for meats and sauces. The original sauce was made in 1686 by two chemists, John W. Lea and William Perrins, in Worcestershire, England. The two men were hired by Lord Sandys to duplicate a sauce he had tasted in India. Sandys gave Lea and Perrins a list of ingredients and asked them to work out the quantities needed to create the sauce. The chemists developed a similar sauce, but neither they nor Sandys were completely satisfied with the results. They stored the sauce and tasted it a few months later. The men discovered that

2. _____

_____

_____

B Practice

Read each set of directions. Write what would come next.

Repotting a Plant

When houseplants become root bound and too small for the pot they are in, choose a pot one size larger than the present one. Fill the bottom with small stones, packing peanuts, or broken pieces of clay pots. Add some potting soil to the bottom of the pot. Tap the plant out of the existing pot.

1. _____

_____

_____

Creating a Tossed Salad

Gather the ingredients you want to use in the salad, such as lettuce, tomatoes, peppers, mushrooms, and salad dressing. Wash the lettuce, and dry it by setting it on a clean towel or some paper towels and patting it. If you have one, a salad spinner could also be used to dry the lettuce. Break the lettuce into bite-sized pieces, and put them in a large salad bowl.

2. _____

_____

_____

Washing a Car

Use warm, not hot, water and a special cleaning product for cars. Use a hose or bucket and a sponge or rags.

3. _____

_____

_____

Painting a Room

Choose the paint color to be used. Gather the painting equipment you will need. Spread a drop cloth on the floor to protect it from drips and spills. After painting the ceiling, begin at a corner near the ceiling. Paint a three-inch strip on the wall just below the ceiling.

4. _____

_____

_____

C ▸ Apply

**Read each situation. Write three possible outcomes. Circle the outcome
you think would be most likely and explain why you chose that outcome.**

An experienced mountain climber has faced many obstacles in attempting to climb a
difficult peak and now a storm is on the way.

1. a. _____

   b. _____

   c. _____

2. _____

   _____

On a seemingly pleasant spring day, a family with five children plans a day's outing in the
woods not far from their home. They plan to hike for a while and then eat a picnic lunch.

3. a. _____

   b. _____

   c. _____

4. _____

   _____

A business executive works for weeks on a presentation. Hurrying to work on the day of
the big event, the executive encounters a series of mishaps. At last the time comes for her
presentation.

5. a. _____

   b. _____

   c. _____

6. _____

   _____

Predict the outcomes. Answer each question by circling the most logical prediction.

While exploring a cave, with their teacher, some young spelunkers make some incredible discoveries. On the walls are drawings of animals. The drawings look very old. They also discover some fossilized human remains.

1. What are the spelunkers likely to do?

   A They will report the find to a university anthropology department.

   B They will remove the bones and give them to a museum.

   C They will charge admission for others to go in the cave and see the wonders.

   D They will keep the discovery a secret.

A number of foreign plants and animals thrive in Florida. Usually they got to Florida on ships or in luggage. The Siamese catfish is one example. These fish crawl out of Florida canals. The Brazilian water hyacinth is another example. These plants choke Florida waterways. South American piranhas sometimes escape into local waters. Most of these nonnative plants and animals cause problems.

2. What should the people in Florida do?

   F They should look for better ways to use the nonnative plants and animals so that they help, not hurt Florida.

   G They should prevent more plants and animals from coming in and find ways to safely eliminate the ones that are already there.

   H They should spray everywhere with poison to kill the unwanted pests.

   J They should ask people not to bring new plants and animals to Florida.

A volunteer group has as its goal providing affordable housing for low-income people. Individuals and groups can volunteer to work on houses being built. Ed wants to help build a house but he can't do physical labor.

3. How will Ed help?

   A Ed will help pass laws that allow the houses to be sold for a high price.

   B Ed will donate money and materials.

   C Ed will pay people to give money.

   D Ed will take a carpentry class.

A reader who enjoys sailing to many places was asked to choose a favorite work of literature and to present a report about it to a local literary society.

4. Which book is the reader likely to choose?

   F Jill Ker Conway's *The Road from Coorain,* an essay that describes the Australian landscape.

   G Stephen Crane's "The Open Boat," a story about experiences in a lifeboat after a ship is sunk.

   H Joseph Conrad's *Heart of Darkness,* the story of a boat trip up the Congo.

   J Paul Theroux's *The Old Patagonian Express,* a book about a train trip from Boston to the tip of Argentina.

Identifying Fact and Opinion

A **fact** is a statement that can be tested and proved. *George Washington was the first President of the United States.* This statement is a fact. It can be proved.

An **opinion** tells how a person thinks or feels about something. Opinions cannot be proved. *George Washington was the greatest president.* This statement is an opinion. Some words, such as *it seems, I think, greatest, terrible, should,* and *wonderful* may signal opinions.

Read each statement. Write *fact* or *opinion*. Circle any word that signals an opinion.

1. Yesterday was a lovely day. _____

2. The plot of the new children's movie centers around a cuddly mouse children will adore. _____

3. Ansel Adams was famous for his photographs of the American Southwest. _____

4. The Statue of Liberty is located on an island. _____

5. In the 1830s, San Francisco was a small village of about 800 people. _____

6. Everyone should vote because it is important to the country. _____

7. Statistics can be both impressive and misleading. _____

8. I love snowy days. _____

9. It would cost more to repair the fire station than to replace it. _____

10. More Americans died at the battle of Gettysburg than in any other battle in American history. _____

11. Wonderful views of the city can be seen from the Washington Monument. _____

12. Without question, computers make all writing and organizing tasks easier. _____

13. Ranchers often graze cattle on public land. _____

14. The castles of Spain are the most unique of all the European castles. _____

B Practice

If a passage contains an opinion, underline the opinion. If the passage contains only facts, circle the passage.

1. Faults, or cracks, in the earth's surface can run through land and under the ocean. Undersea faults can create powerful ocean waves. Some people call these tidal waves. They shouldn't use this term, however, because the waves have nothing to do with tides. Scientists use the Japanese word *tsunami*, which mean "harbor wave," as the term for a huge wave created by the movement of undersea faults.

2. Monticello in Virginia was Thomas Jefferson's home. He designed the house himself, basing it on classical architecture. After all, classical architecture is the best model of harmony and proportion. The Temple of Vesta in Rome inspired the columned porticos Jefferson used at Monticello.

3. Authors such as Charles Dickens protested child labor conditions in British factories. Unregulated child labor existed in British factories until the middle of the 19th century. The Factory Act of 1847 limited a child's work day in textile mills to 10 hours.

4. There is a new kind of addiction. The addiction is to computers. Some people can't seem to pull themselves away from the computer. They can sit in front of the machine for five hours, and it may seem to them like five minutes. One sign of addiction to the computer is that a person sneaks around to use one—just like other addicts.

5. For some European settlers, hearing Native American words was an educational experience. They learned new words for rivers, animals, plants, and mountains. Settlers in cities and villages were wise to name their settlements using the beautiful Native American words.

6. George Orwell is the name used by author Eric Arthur Blair. One of his famous novels, *Animal Farm,* is a satire of Stalinism. This novel is his best. He also wrote *1984,* a novel that contains the well-known warning "Big Brother is watching you."

C ▸ Apply

Read each topic. Write one fact and one opinion about the topic.

A Sport

1. Fact _____

    _____

2. Opinion _____

    _____

A Movie

3. Fact _____

    _____

4. Opinion _____

    _____

A Food

5. Fact _____

    _____

6. Opinion _____

    _____

A Season

7. Fact _____

    _____

8. Opinion _____

    _____

A President

9. Fact _____

    _____

10. Opinion _____

    _____

Circle the answer that shows whether the statement is a *fact* or an *opinion*.

1. Gwendolyn Brooks, an African-American poet, grew up on the South side of Chicago.

    A fact

    B opinion

2. The Florida panther is a beautiful and critically endangered mammal whose only hope of survival is a captive breeding program.

    C fact

    D opinion

3. Although traditional Chinese medicine is an ancient science, unfortunately many Westerners are unfamiliar with it.

    F fact

    G opinion

4. Today's CD-ROM technology permits whole libraries to be stored on a single disk, thus allowing rapid access to information.

    H fact

    J opinion

5. Overpopulation is one problem that an increasing number of nations will surely face unless drastic measures are taken now.

    A fact

    B opinion

6. Perhaps the world's most famous and most beautiful example of a coral reef is the Great Barrier Reef in Australia.

    C fact

    D opinion

7. Airbags, which inflate automatically during an accident, can only be used once.

    F fact

    G opinion

8. Although Eleanor Roosevelt was the wife of Franklin Delano Roosevelt, she became famous for her own achievements.

    H fact

    J opinion

9. The Library of Congress, the world's largest library, holds millions of items and has exhibition areas that display items of historical significance.

    A fact

    B opinion

10. Leonardo da Vinci's painting of the mysterious Mona Lisa is his best work.

    C fact

    D opinion

Identifying Fact and Opinion

A **fact** is a statement that tells something that can be proved. An **opinion** expresses judgments, feelings, or beliefs, none of which can be proved. Some opinions are based on emotion or bias. Words such as *wonderful*, *best*, or *silly* signal this kind of opinion. An opinion that is supported by some evidence is called a valid opinion.

Read the following sentences. Then write *fact* or *opinion* on the line. For each opinion, write *biased* or *valid*.

1. Many people think the Victorians lived by a rigid moral code. Books about the period show that this was only partly true.

   _____

2. The polar bear can rightly be called the King of the North. Polar bears are the largest land predators in the North. So a grown polar bear fears no other animal.

   _____

3. The cowhand of the Old West had borrowed many ideas from the Mexican vaquero. The Texas saddle, however, with a pommel for the rider's lariat, was a vast improvement over Mexican saddle design.

   _____

4. During the last ten seconds, your brains absorbed ten million bits of data. You will forget most of this information immediately, but you may remember some of it all your life.

   _____

5. There is a simple way to reduce garbage in landfills. Few people realize that 40 percent of landfills are made up of paper. Recycling paper can help a lot and is a simple process.

   _____

6. Hong Kong is a city of contrasts. Ancient and modern architecture exist side by side. Interesting Chinese junks and lumbering ferries sail the harbor.

   _____

B Practice

These statements are opinions. Rewrite them so they express only facts.

1. Cole Porter, the most famous American songwriter, was so depressed by the failure of his first musical that he foolishly joined the Foreign Legion.

   _____

   _____

   _____

   _____

2. Historians have been unable to verify the silly but popular legend that Betsy Ross made the first flag at the request of a special committee that included the brilliant general, George Washington.

   _____

   _____

   _____

   _____

3. Everyone has heard of the Baseball Hall of Fame, which is located in Cooperstown, New York. In the 1970s, a long overdue special committee was set up to consider admitting players from the Negro Leagues.

   _____

   _____

   _____

   _____

4. Marian Anderson was a famous African-American singer of her day. Her most famous and most brilliantly performed concert took place in front of the Lincoln Memorial.

   _____

   _____

   _____

   _____

C ▸ Apply

Read each topic. Write a fact and an opinion about the topic.

A Song

1. Fact _____

   _____

2. Opinion _____

   _____

A Vacation

3. Fact _____

   _____

4. Opinion _____

   _____

A Car

5. Fact _____

   _____

6. Opinion _____

   _____

A Job

7. Fact _____

   _____

8. Opinion _____

   _____

A Dog

9. Fact _____

   _____

10. Opinion _____

   _____

Circle the answer that shows whether the statement is a *fact* or an *opinion*.

1. At one time, George Washington Carver was the only agricultural chemist interested in the peanut.

   A fact

   B opinion

2. A whale pod is a wonderful support system in which whale family members care for one another.

   C fact

   D opinion

3. Working from home using computers and other electronic equipment is the ideal way to work.

   F fact

   G opinion

4. Sir Arthur Conan Doyle wrote 56 stories about the fictional detective Sherlock Holmes.

   H fact

   J opinion

5. You will find the markets of Cairo, Egypt, attractive because of the strange wares that are offered.

   A fact

   B opinion

6. There is no better book about two generations of women than Amy Tan's *The Joy Luck Club*.

   C fact

   D opinion

7. The rhyming books by Theodor Seuss Geisel, known as Dr. Seuss, are favorites of many young children.

   F fact

   G opinion

8. One of the sights that should not be missed on any trip to England is Stonehenge.

   H fact

   J opinion

9. San Francisco was originally founded by the Spanish as Yerba Buena in 1776.

   A fact

   B opinion

10. Freedom of speech and other of our most cherished civil liberties are guaranteed in the Bill of Rights of the Constitution.

    C fact

    D opinion

 **Read On** As you read "Trapped by Fear," identify facts and opinions. Then answer the questions.

Recognizing Author's Purpose

Authors write for a variety of purposes. Some of the more common **author's purposes** for writing include to entertain, to inform, to persuade or express an opinion, to describe, and to explain or instruct.

The box lists different forms of writing. Write each form under the purpose for which it would likely have been written.

| recipe | newspaper | joke | store catalog | travel brochure |
| story | textbook | ad | newsmagazine | letter to the editor |

to entertain

1. _____

2. _____

to inform

3. _____

4. _____

to persuade or express an opinion

5. _____

6. _____

to describe

7. _____

8. _____

to explain or instruct

9. _____

10. _____

B Practice

Circle the answer that shows the author's purpose for writing each passage.

1. Tangy sea breezes drift through Easton. Vacationers love Easton's grassy parks and seaside play.

   A to entertain

   B to inform

   C to describe

   D to explain or instruct

2. Competition is what made this country great. Big companies are big because they're doing something right. Government should leave them alone to do business any way they want.

   F to inform

   G to express an opinion

   H to describe

   J to explain or instruct

3. Why do bees sometimes leave their old home for a new one? The reason may be that their old home is too crowded. There may not be enough room for bees to store all the honey they need for food.

   A to entertain

   B to inform

   C to persuade

   D to describe

4. Football practice at Bear Creek High had finally come to an end. The team, weakened by injuries, faced its toughest opponents of the season the next day. Jeff Watson felt his chest tighten and wondered if he was going to have an asthma attack.

   F to entertain

   G to inform

   H to describe

   J to explain or instruct

5. The first schools were founded in Sumer, an area that is now the country of Iraq. Sumerians also invented writing by scratching words into soft clay tablets. The tablets were then dried in the sun until they became hard as stone.

   A to entertain

   B to express an opinion

   C to describe

   D to explain or instruct

6. There are times when the night sky glows with bands of color. The bands may begin as cloud shapes and then spread into a great arc across the entire sky. They may fall in folds like a curtain drawn across the heavens. The sky glows with yellow, pink, green, violet, blue, and red. These lights are called the aurora borealis in the Northern Hemisphere.

   F to entertain

   G to express an opinion

   H to describe

   J to explain or instruct

7. In the middle of October 1812, Napoleon's army was forced to withdraw from Moscow. A fire had destroyed French supplies there, making it impossible for the army to stay through the winter.

   A to entertain

   B to inform

   C to persuade

   D to describe

C ▶ Apply

Read the scenarios. Identify what the person will write and for what purpose—to entertain, to inform, to persuade or express an opinion, to describe, or to explain or instruct.

At the picnic, many people complimented Mrs. Holt on her taco salad. They asked her how to make the delicious dish. What might Mrs. Holt write and for what purpose?

1. She will write _____

2. Her purpose for writing is _____

In the GED class, the instructor asked each person to choose a favorite historical person from the 20th century and to write about that person.

3. Each member of the class will write _____

   _____

4. Their purpose for writing is _____

Ms. Martinez was irate as she read the local paper. The town council planned to raise taxes, and no one seemed to be complaining or to understand that there were reasons why an increase would be difficult for some people.

5. She will write _____

   _____

6. Her purpose for writing is _____

   _____

Denny wanted to be a stand-up comedian, and the upcoming community talent show would give him an opportunity to practice his skill.

7. He will write _____

8 His purpose for writing is _____

Art's favorite state was Wisconsin. He visited the state often and was asked by a local newspaper to write what can be seen there during each season of the year.

9. He will write _____

10. His purpose for writing is _____

   _____

Read each passage. On the line, write the author's purpose for writing the passage. Use the list in the box to help you.

to entertain	to explain or instruct
to inform	to describe
to persuade or express an opinion	

1. Molds are important types of fungi. They can be found on breads, cheeses, and overripe fruit. They are formed when small airborne organisms find a suitable nutrient source to grow on. Scientists have discovered many practical uses for molds. Some cheeses are ripened by the action of the fungi. Penicillin, a mold, has saved millions of lives.

   _____

2. Chocolate! Forget it! As delicious as it may be, there are many reasons it should be avoided. Here are some of them. Chocolate is high in fat. Chocolate can be addictive. Chocolate contains ingredients that can make people feel nervous. Need I say more? Stay away from the stuff.

   _____

3. Have you ever stacked two glasses only to discover later that they are stuck together when you want to use them? A simple way to separate them is to hold them under a stream of hot water or to place them in a sink full of hot water. The glasses will expand because of the heat and can be separated.

   _____

4. Wind pushes huge clouds across the vast desert. The ever-present dust of the dry earth hangs in the air and turns the sky from yellow to orange and from red to purple as the clouds refract the light.

   _____

5. She wasn't afraid of Black Diamond even if he was a rather high-strung and nervous horse. He was used to living in the wilds, so it would all take time; but Cynthia knew this when she made the bet with her father. He gave her three days to make friends with the horse. He gave her one month after that to ride him around the corral.

   _____

6. The rain forest has a feature unique to it—the canopy. The canopy is a kind of cover of vegetation. It is the canopy that holds in the moisture necessary for the many kinds of plant and animal life that live on the floor of the rain forest.

   _____

A Introduce

Identifying Author's Purpose

An **author's purpose** is the reason or goal an author has for writing. There are many purposes for writing. These are some of them:

> to entertain   to inform   to describe
> to explain or instruct   to persuade or express an opinion

Sometimes an author may have more than one reason for writing. As you read, ask yourself what kind of writing you are reading. This may give you a clue to the author's purpose or purposes.

For each writing form, identify two purposes an author might have.

short story

1. _____

2. _____

magazine article

3. _____

4. _____

TV commercial

5. _____

6. _____

newspaper editorial

7. _____

8. _____

textbook

9. _____

10. _____

poem

11. _____

12. _____

B Practice

Read each passage. Write the purpose or purposes the author may have had for writing the passage. Choose from among these:

> to entertain   to inform   to describe
> to explain or instruct   to persuade or express an opinion

1. Use a comma between the main clauses in a compound sentence. Place a comma before a coordinating conjunction that joins two main clauses.

   _____

2. Many sounds are common to a large number of languages. Nevertheless, languages do not all have the same sounds or the same number of sounds.

   _____

3. From 1964 to 1997, the size of the average farm has increased while the number of people working on farms has decreased. This is a problem that must be addressed if we want to be assured of a reliable food supply.

   _____

4. Suddenly there came a clap of thunder. It was an angry, metallic sound. A mighty wind arose and filled the air with dust. Palm trees swayed, and the birds were silent.

   _____

5. In contrast to the rest of the house, the living room was a mess. Inspector Tuttle viewed the scene, walking carefully through the debris of what had once been furniture. Something had happened. This was one mystery he intended to solve.

   _____

6. Of all the travel magazines on the market today, the one I want to recommend is *Hit the Road*. Interesting articles about exotic destinations will grab your attention and make your reading an enjoyable experience.

   _____

C Apply

Complete each statement with one of the purposes for writing listed here: *entertain, inform, persuade or express an opinion, describe, explain or instruct.*

1. If you had a great idea for a story based on amusing events in your own life, your purpose for writing would be to

   _____

2. If you wanted to tell your neighbor how to remove a carpet stain, your purpose for writing would be to

   _____

3. If, in a letter to a friend, you wanted to tell about the beautiful landscape in the place you visited, your purpose for writing would be to

   _____

4. If you wanted to write a letter to your senator about an issue you felt strongly about, your purpose for writing would be to

   _____

5. If you were asked by your boss to write a report about the sales your team has made, your purpose for writing would be to

   _____

6. If your friend asked you for a copy of your favorite recipe for baked beans, your purpose for writing would be to

   _____

7. If you wanted to write a poem about the antics of your pet dog, your purpose for writing would be to

   _____

8. If you were asked to write a magazine article about a favorite bird, your purpose for writing would be to

   _____

9. If you wanted to list some reasons why you should find a way to recycle more trash, your purpose for writing would be to

   _____

10. If you were asked to tell what a painting purchased by the local art museum looks like, your purpose for writing would be to

    _____

D Check Up

Circle the answer that shows the author's purpose for writing each passage.

1. Parakeets were first discovered in Australia in 1805. It was not until 1840 that live ones were first taken to England. As time went on, more and more parakeets were shipped away. Wild parakeets were shipped to the United States from Australia and Europe. In 1884, the Australian government passed a law to stop shipments of parakeets from leaving the country.

   A to entertain

   B to inform

   C to persuade

   D to describe

2. Today was the day the ship would arrive from Earth. Novina was anxious to talk with the people from the mother planet. Sometimes she could not believe the stories her parents told her about Earth. But what made this ship truly special was the gifts it would bring.

   F to entertain

   G to express an opinion

   H to describe

   J to explain or instruct

3. Packing for a trip? Whether a weekend trip or a month-long excursion, there are certain steps to follow when packing.

   A to entertain

   B to describe

   C to persuade

   D to explain or instruct

4. The towering, twisted tree stood weirdly on rows of great legs. It was a strangler fig. The tallest, yet strangest, tree in the forest.

   F to entertain

   G to persuade

   H to describe

   J to explain or instruct

5. Gum can easily be removed from carpet using an ice cube. Hold the ice cube on the gum. When the gum hardens, scrape the gum off the carpet with a knife.

   A to entertain

   B to describe

   C to persuade

   D to explain or instruct

6. George Washington, the first United States president, was born in Virginia on February 22, 1732. As a young man, he became a surveyor. At the age of 21, he became an officer in the British Army. He fought bravely in battles against the French and the Indians. His fame as a soldier spread.

   F to entertain

   G to express an opinion

   H to inform

   J to describe

7. If it were up to me, I would make "God Bless America" or "America the Beautiful" our national anthem. Either song would be much easier to sing than the current anthem.

   A to entertain

   B to inform

   C to express an opinion

   D to describe

Recognizing Author's Point of View

When an author writes a story, an article, a poem, or a play, he or she has certain views or biases about the characters or topic.

An **author's point of view** may be positive or negative. For example, a restaurant critic may give a glowing review of a new cafe. Or an editor may express a negative opinion in an editorial about the mayor's proposed tax increase.

Sometimes an author's point of view is clearly expressed. Other times it must be inferred from the tone and the choice of words the author uses.

Write *positive* or *negative* to show the author's point of view toward the subject. Then write *stated* or *implied* to tell how you know what the author's point of view is.

The state of Alaska is without question our most beautiful state. Its towering peaks, abundant wildlife, and unspoiled wilderness are without equal.

1. _____

2. _____

The latest toy craze to hit the shelves for the upcoming holiday season is the Mad Bull. Does any child really need a toy whose main purpose is to make snorting noises? What is the fascination? Perhaps its goal is to be as repulsive as possible. If so, it succeeds.

3. _____

4. _____

Longing for a cruise of a lifetime? You'll want to try the Ice Queen. It will seem like a lifetime by the time you get off. Short on staff and long on overheated cabins, this ship will take you on an endurance cruise you won't soon forget. And the food— bring your own or suffer the consequences of the so-called delicacies put before you.

5. _____

6. _____

Mayor Simpkins—three cheers! The new tax plan will create the revenue needed to repair the crumbling city infrastructure, give pay raises to the police, open more shelters, and pave more streets. This unpopular, but long-needed plan, demonstrates that our mayor is a politician with leadership skills.

7. _____

8. _____

B ▶ Practice

Read each passage. Then circle the answer for each question.

Native Americans called it the Land of the Burning Mountains. The rivers, they said, ran hot on the bottom. Fountains of steam and water shot out of the earth, high into the air. Hot mud, like pink, yellow, and brown paint, flowed from springs in the ground. Pools of boiling water would wash clothes clean in minutes.

It wasn't until 1870 that white people explored the amazing Land of the Burning Mountains. They came back wide-eyed. They demanded that it be preserved forever as a great park for the people of the United States. Two years later, Congress set the region apart from nearby lands and called it Yellowstone National Park. That is how the wonderful National Park Service came about. Today there are more than 80 magnificent parks. They are controlled by the United States Department of the Interior.

1. The writer uses words that
   A are neutral
   B suggest good things about mud springs
   C suggest bad things about national parks
   D suggest good things about national parks

2. The author seems to be
   F for national parks
   G against Yellowstone National Park
   H against the Department of the Interior
   J not taking sides

Falconry originated in China as early as 2200 B.C. The Chinese gave trained falcons as gifts. The "sport" of falconry reached England in the fourth and fifth centuries.

A bird that was used in falconry was either taken from the nest when it was still young or trapped when it had become full grown. Next, the glorious wild bird had to be bent to the falconer's will. Once it had hunted for food. Now it had to catch the prey that its master wished to hunt for sport.

3. The writer uses words that
   A are neutral
   B suggest bad things about falcons
   C suggest good things about falconers
   D suggest bad things about falconry

4. The author seems to be
   F for falconry
   G against falconry
   H for falconers
   J not taking sides

210

C ▶ Apply

Write *positive* or *negative* to describe the author's point of view. Then follow the directions.

Of all the farm animals a person can own, the goat makes the best pet.

1. _____

2. Underline the word that tells you what the author's point of view is.

In Peru, there once lived the most peace-loving Indians ever known. These people were the Inca.

3. _____

4. Underline the phrases that tell you what the author's point of view is.

The sly coyote that chatters and howls from lonely western hillsides is boasting of another cruel victory over American farmers.

5. _____

6. Underline three words that tell you what the author's point of view is.

Boston can be delightful on a summer Saturday. Many people have fled to Cape Cod or Martha's Vineyard. The city isn't crowded and getting around is easy.

7. _____

8. Underline the sentence or sentences that explain why the author holds the point of view he or she does.

Far from being romantic or exciting, life on a sailing ship of the past was, at best, difficult. Conditions on board were unhealthy, food was often rotten or rancid, and quarters were cramped.

9. _____

10. Underline the words that help describe the author's point of view.

Some baseball teams have a special award for good plays. Dodger manager Wilbert Robinson came up with a "Bonehead Club" for players who committed bonehead mistakes. Perhaps such an award should be established for our current "professional" baseball team. The award might inspire—or embarrass—the players into better performances.

11. _____

12. Underline the sentences that tell you what the author's point of view is.

Read each passage. Then circle the answer for each question.

In Boston, Copley Square is often full of young people with their shoes off, sitting under the trees beside Trinity Church. This architectural masterpiece sits between two other remarkable buildings. One is the Hancock Tower, a modern slice of reflecting glass. The other is the postmodern New England Building. Its design somehow combines humor and dignity. Other young people wander through the park or the Common or enjoy window shopping along Charles Street.

1. The author uses words that make Boston seem

    A much like any other city

    B uncomfortably hot in July

    C like a nice place to visit

    D more expensive than other cities

In 1519 the richest and most powerful ruler in North America was the Aztec emperor Montezuma II. He called himself Emperor of the World and ruled from a great palace in Mexico City. Then a man named Cortés was sent to explore and open trade. He decided, however, to conquer Aztec lands, collect treasure, and force Montezuma to obey the Spanish crown. That was like a mouse giving orders to a lion.

2. In the last sentence, the author suggests that

    F Cortés was a brave warrior

    G Cortés was basically a shy man

    H Montezuma was greater than Cortés

    J Montezuma had no patience with foreigners

Do you believe in flying saucers? Many claims about sightings of flying saucers can easily be explained. The "invasion" of Farmington, New Mexico, was one of the most dramatic, yet explained, flying saucer scares. The "saucers" began flying at about 10:15 A.M. They soon filled the air. It turned out that a large balloon had been sent aloft several hours earlier from a nearby air force base. In the cold air, the balloon had burst into hundreds of tiny pieces of plastic. These shone in the sun as they floated over the town.

3. The author's point of view seems to suggest that

    A flying saucers are real

    B people are usually fooled by hoaxes

    C balloons are flying saucers

    D saucer sightings are explainable

During the 1530s, Spanish explorer Francisco Coronado first heard about Cibola. According to legend, Cibola was a land north of Mexico that had seven cities filled with gold, silver, and jewels. Coronado sent a priest named Fra Marcos de Niza to explore what is now New Mexico. After hearing Niza's reports, Coronado led an expedition to the area. But he never found any riches in the villages. For centuries, other explorers and adventurers have all attempted the same foolish quest that Coronado did.

4. The author's point of view about Cibola seems to be that

    F explorers have looked in the wrong places

    G all the gold was removed by the natives

    H the city as it was described, never existed

    J Cibola will someday be found

Identifying Author's Point of View

Writers hold a **point of view** about the subjects they write about. However, writers do not always state their motives for writing nor do they always directly state their beliefs or feelings.

A writer's point of view may be positive, negative, or neutral. Writing must be evaluated to determine if the information is accurate and the conclusions are reasonable.

To express a particular point of view, a writer sometimes uses words with a positive connotation, such as *curious,* or a negative connotation, such as *nosy.* Watch for the language writers use. Their choice of words is sometimes a clue to their point of view.

Each numbered word has a positive connotation. Change the word to one with a negative connotation. Use words from the box.

odd	cramped	stubborn	bookish	cheap
difficult	skinny	old	dull	garish

1. peaceful _____

2. cozy _____

3. mature _____

4. frugal _____

5. persistent _____

6. colorful _____

7. studious _____

8. slim _____

9. unique _____

10. challenging _____

Each numbered word has a negative connotation. Change the word to one with a positive connotation. Use words from the box.

well-fed	cabin	well-used	helpful	controlled
refreshing	determined	frugal	shining	ignorant

11. glaring _____

12. fat _____

13. stingy _____

14. ragged _____

15. dumb _____

16. bone-chilling _____

17. hardhearted _____

18. shack _____

19. merciless _____

20. pushy _____

B Practice

Read the passage. Follow the directions. Answer the questions.

Do you ever wonder why women make poor newscasters and political candidates? It may be that people are uncomfortable when women speak. Their harsh tones may jar people's eardrums. Harsh tones come from tension in the throat and jaw. Tension tightens muscles. Relaxed muscles are essential to a deep, pleasing tone. Tension shows up more in higher-pitched voices. That's why women tend to sound more shrill than men.

1. Circle each statement that is probably an actual fact.

   A Deep tones are pleasing.

   B Relaxed muscles make deep tones.

   C Tension tightens muscles.

2. What is the author's point of view?

   A Women have more relaxed voices than men.

   B Women are more tense than men.

   C Women make poor public speakers because their voices sound shrill.

3. Is the point of view the author holds valid based on facts? If so, why? If not, why not?

   _____

   _____

   _____

4. Why might the passage be considered slanted?

   _____

   _____

5. Is the author's point of view positive, negative, or neutral? Toward whom or what?

   _____

   _____

C ▶ Apply

Rewrite each passage twice. First use words and phrases that reflect a positive point of view. Then use words that reflect a negative point of view.

The food at Cafe Main Street is _____, _____, and _____. A trip to this neighborhood restaurant is _____.

1. _____

_____

_____

2. _____

_____

_____

Congressman Joseph is a _____, _____, _____ politician. He _____ be reelected this fall.

3. _____

_____

_____

4. _____

_____

_____

To many people, the most important part of a pizza is the crust. Those who like thin crust will get a pizza _____.

5. _____

_____

_____

6. _____

_____

_____

Read each paragraph and circle the answer for each question.

The coyote has been hunted more than any other pest. Every trick that people know has been used in the long battle to do away with the coyote. Fifty to a hundred thousand are eliminated each year in the United States. However, the cruel coyote is holding its own. In fact, it has spread from its point of origin in the prairies and mountains of the West to many new areas. Today, at least two million roam the western United States looking for an innocent lamb or some unsuspecting chickens.

1. The information is

    A   balanced

    B   slanted for coyotes

    C   slanted against coyotes

    D   slanted against farmers

2. By writing this passage, the author wanted to

    F   describe the coyote

    G   persuade other people to tolerate the coyote

    H   persuade people to dislike the coyote

    J   explain the ecology of the coyote

Smokey the Bear did his job too well. At one time, firefighters rushed to put out every wildfire. Now the Forest Service may send just one firefighter to answer the alarm. He or she may suggest that the fire go on burning because it is a "good" fire. Some kinds of pine trees would die out unless there were fires. Their seeds are glued inside the cones with resin. It takes fire to melt the resin and let the seeds pop out. Good, small fires help prevent bigger fires.

3. What does the author suggest in this passage?

    A   The Forest Service has fired too many firefighters.

    B   Some fires help certain trees grow.

    C   Lightning causes the greatest number of fires.

    D   Resin burns at very low temperatures.

4. The author's point of view sees to be

    F   in favor of letting small fires burn

    G   against letting small fires burn

    H   for letting large fires burn

    J   not taking sides

Making Generalizations

Writers sometimes make statements that present conclusions that apply to many people, facts, events, or situations. These statements are called **generalizations.** Generalizations can sum up what has been said or introduce what will be said.

Certain words can introduce or signal generalizations. Some common ones are *most, many, few, all, usually, generally, typically.* Not all generalizations, however, include a signal word.

Put an X in front of each statement that is a generalization.

_____ 1. For many senior citizens, a pet helps ease the loneliness they feel.

_____ 2. Many paragraphs are written so they are gender-neutral, avoiding sexism by using neutral language.

_____ 3. In dry weather, grass turns brown and may be damaged by frequent or improper mowing.

_____ 4. At our local mall, the two largest stores are at either end and are called "anchors."

_____ 5. Most cats are less friendly to humans than dogs.

_____ 6. Television programs for children are usually scheduled during morning and late afternoon hours.

_____ 7. Typically, first-time parents are nervous about handling their new baby and have many questions about what to do.

_____ 8. The new hotel, which will be opened in the spring of next year, will have more rooms than any other in the hotel's chain.

_____ 9. Not all foods at fast-food restaurants are unhealthy or bad for you.

_____ 10. The main character in the latest novel I just read reminds me a lot of myself as a young person.

_____ 11. All computers can be used for design work, allowing the operator to create graphics and other pieces of art.

_____ 12. Most stories have happy endings and satisfying conclusions.

Underline a generalization in each passage.

1. Usually, diseases affect only a few people in a limited area. However, the bubonic plague swept across much of the world in the 14th century. Entire families died of it. Doctors who tried to treat patients often caught the disease and died themselves. In London alone, one hundred thousand people died. Fifty thousand died in Paris. In all, one in every four persons in Europe died of the plague.

2. Few monster stories have staying power that matches that of the Loch Ness monster. The Loch Ness monster is the most widely discussed "sea monster" in the world. The home of the "beast" is northern Scotland. Loch Ness is a narrow body of fresh water more than 20 miles long and about a mile and a half wide. The first report of the Loch Ness monster was made 400 years ago. That sighting was mentioned in a document now kept in a museum in Switzerland. More recent sightings began in large numbers in the early 1930s.

3. Modern paintings and books containing brainteasers are not the only places in which you will find optical illusions. They also exist naturally. One natural optical illusion is the mirage. Almost everyone has seen some movie in which a thirsty desert traveler thinks he or she sees a pool of cool water in the distance and then finds that he or she has imagined it. That's a mirage. Mirages are caused by the bending of light rays.

4. It is a law of life that animals that eat plants are hunted by animals that eat meat. Plant eaters become the source of food for other animals. The zebra and the gazelle, for example, are food for lions. In the same way, the plant-eating dinosaurs were the prey of the meat-eating dinosaurs. Skeletons of dinosaurs have been found that show the teeth marks made by meat-eating dinosaurs. Most experts believe there can be no question how such animals died.

5. It goes without saying that there are many ordinary things we can do on Earth that are impossible to do in outer space. One very simple example is scratching an itch. You couldn't do this if you were wearing a space suit. So how do astronauts scratch their noses if they get an itch while walking on the moon, for instance? Well, the scientists at NASA worked on a solution to this very special problem. Today, built into every astronaut's helmet is a special nose scratcher that can be activated by pressing a button.

6. Many people in the United States buy Buick cars and many people also bathe in Buick bathtubs. The Buick, named after designer David Buick, was the first car made by General Motors. David Buick didn't start out in the car business, however. He was a plumber by trade, and designing new materials was his hobby. Through his design experiments, Buick found a way to blend porcelain with iron. This mixture was strong and useful in bathroom fixtures. One thing that his invention was used for was the porcelain bathtub.

Apply

Write a generalization that could be drawn from information in each passage.

In many books, there are major and minor character. Minor characters may appear on only a few pages, but they can play a key role in the plot. Because authors do not include characters that serve no purpose, studying minor characters can be as interesting and challenging as studying any major or main character.

1. _____

_____

_____

Have you ever seen a television program with an unhappy ending? Have you ever seen a movie in which everything didn't turn out all right for the hero or heroine? Rarely do television shows or movies end sadly or badly. Why? Viewers don't like it when the ending is less than satisfying or happy. They want the "good guys" to win.

2. _____

_____

_____

The bald eagle is the national emblem of the United States. Because of its strong and regal appearance, this bird makes an impressive emblem. Not so long ago, the great bald eagle was on the verge of extinction. For years, the eagle had been hunted for sport. Then the government outlawed the killing of bald eagles. Anyone caught hunting them could be sent to jail.

3. _____

_____

_____

Some animals such as elephants, bears, and buffaloes force old members of their group to leave. These old exiles or hermits, that have been cast off by the herd are often ornery and mean and may attack humans if they are provoked. Lions, tigers, and leopards that are too old to hunt other animals successfully may attack humans as a last resort.

4. _____

_____

_____

D Check Up

Circle the statement that would be a generalization based on each passage.

1. One of the greatest rulers of all time was called Charlemagne. He was a medieval French king who became the first Holy Roman Emperor. Charlemagne was noted for his extraordinary size and strength. He was six feet four inches tall, and he weighed 275 pounds. It was said that he was capable of killing a man with one blow of his fist, and he was considered the best rider and hunter in the realm.

    A Charlemagne was a great leader.

    B Charlemagne was tall and strong.

    C Most people were smaller and weaker than Charlemagne.

    D Charlemagne was the ruler of the Holy Roman Empire.

2. How much sugar have you had today? Maybe more than you think. Soft drinks, candy, and pastries, of course, contain a great deal of sugar. But so do foods such as catsup, frozen dinners, salad dressing, hot dogs, and packaged bread. Sugar is added to those foods when they are processed. So the average American eats about one hundred pounds of sugar each year.

    F Americans eat too much sugar.

    G Catsup and hot dogs are unexpected sources of sugar.

    H Americans should not eat processed foods.

    J Usually, processed foods have lots of sugar in them.

3. When do you cry? People cry for joy at weddings and births. They cry at funerals and when feeling sorry for themselves. Crying actually makes a person feel better, so if you feel a good cry coming on—go right ahead.

    A People cry for many reasons.

    B Crying is healthy.

    C People shed tears when they cry.

    D Typically, only humans shed tears.

4. Inventions have interesting and sometimes unusual names. For instance, the saxophone was invented by Joseph Sax. Thomas Blanket set up a loom in 1340 and wove the first blanket. When you eat a sandwich, you are indulging in a treat made popular by the Earl of Sandwich. If you've ever ridden a Ferris wheel, you owe the thrilling experience to George Washington Ferris, who built the first one.

    F Many objects are named for their inventors.

    G No one used covers before Blanket.

    H Generally all new inventions are important.

    J All inventions are given the inventor's name.

Read On   As you read "Visions of the Night," watch for generalizations. Then answer the questions.

Identifying Style Techniques

Every writer has his or her own unique style of writing. Some writers have such unique styles that a passage of their work could be identified as theirs even when taken out of the work. A writer's style can be as individual as a fingerprint.

There are many techniques authors use to create a style. Some authors may use very long sentences, others short ones. Some authors may use highly descriptive language; others use almost no description. Some authors prefer lots of action; some use mostly dialogue. Other authors use frequent interruptions, creating them by using punctuation such as dashes or colons. Some authors use unusual sentence order. These are some of the many ways an author creates a personal style.

Read each passage. Then circle the answer that identifies the style technique most in evidence.

"The sea is our enemy," Jiya replied.
"How can you say that?" Kino asked. "Your father catches fish from the sea and sells them, and that is how you live."
Jiya shook his head. "The sea is our enemy," he repeated.

1. **A** long sentences

   B dialogue

   C descriptive details

   D short, choppy sentences

It was a great surprise to the people of the west coast of the Spanish Americas when Sir Francis Drake arrived in California on June 17, 1759. We know that when he returned to England, Drake reported to the queen about his travels. One question remains unanswered to this day. That question is, just where did he land in California?

2. **F** long sentences

   G dialogue

   H descriptive details

   J short, choppy sentences

At 5:30 A.M. a pool of yellow light splashes from the kitchen window onto the frosted grass outside. Earl pulls on his work clothes and goes to the barn, which smells of hay and animals. He switches on the radio, turning the volume high. Station WMT at Cedar Rapids offers complete reports on farm prices and good loud music.

3. **A** long sentences

   B dialogue

   C descriptive details

   D short, choppy sentences

Bet was the only passenger for Pagosa. The bus stopped. Bet got off. The bus roared on toward Bayfield. She stood. She looked up and down the street. She wondered why she had come.

4. **F** long sentences

   G dialogue

   H descriptive details

   J short, choppy sentences

B ▸ Practice

Read the description of each author. Then read each passage. Write the label for the author who most likely wrote the passage.

Author A is known for long, flowing sentences packed with action and adventure.

Author B writes using highly descriptive language that paints effective word pictures.

Author C uses dialogue extensively to move the action along and to reveal character traits and feelings.

Author D is known for a writing style that uses short sentences with little description.

Author E has an unusual style of using frequent interruptions in the form of punctuation to make explanations.

Our canoes bucked like broncos as we hit Devil's Channel. Icy spray shot over the gunwales. I glanced toward the canoe bobbing just twenty yards to my left. Jimmy Farnsworth knelt in the bow. His hair fluttered in the stiff breeze. He dug his paddle into the water with more effort than skill. You would have to give him an A for effort. There was no question that he desperately wanted to keep the canoe afloat and was doing everything he could so that it did.

1. _____

"You are always at home or in the office," her friends said to her. "You should go to the theater or the opera."

"But Chad and I have no time to go to theaters," she answered sedately. "Besides, we have no time for nonsense, and neither of us likes opera."

"Still," her friends would reply, "you need some entertainment. You both work too much."

"Nonsense," she answered. "We both thrive on work."

2. _____

Marble—a decorative and durable stone—is prized by sculptors and builders. It is a kind of limestone that has been metamorphosed (changed) through the action of heat far below the earth's surface. The heat has compressed the limestone. The result—the hard, heavy rock known as marble.

3. _____

One sunny day, a fisherman on Lake Michigan struggled with his nets, which were caught on something under the water. He pulled hard, but his nets would not come free. So the next day he and a friend returned to the same spot with scuba gear and plunged beneath the waters to investigate. Far beneath the surface, they stared in amazement at the "something" that had fouled the nets. It was an old sailing ship.

4. _____

C ▸ Apply

Read each passage and identify the style technique using the list in the box to help you. Then write another sentence that continues the passage and uses the same style technique as the passage.

long sentences	dialogue	short sentences
descriptive details	action	interrupting punctuation

Serge was not interested in the snow when he got off the freight train. It was early one evening during the Depression. Serge never even noticed the snow, but he must have felt it seeping down his neck, cold and wet. He must have felt it sopping in his shoes, too; but if you asked him, he wouldn't have known snow was in the air. Even under the bright lights of the main street, Serge didn't see the snowdrifts. He was too hungry, too sleepy, too exhausted.

1. _____

2. _____

_____

I let myself into the dark and quiet apartment, hating to walk into empty rooms. When Mom was home, life wasn't too bad, even though there were just the two of us and Mom worked four days a week. I turned on the hall light because I can't stand the dark. In front of me was Mom's sewing table strewn with cloth and patterns, and her sewing box sat on one of the chairs. I wondered why she had left such a mess when normally she is a very neat person.

3. _____

4. _____

_____

"The computer. For the last time, turn it off and go to bed."
"You don't understand, Mom. There are five of us talking in a chat room. The conversation is really getting interesting. I don't want to stop now to go to bed, for pete's sake. Please—just 15 minutes more."
My mother's face gave me my answer. I logged off.
"There'll be other interesting discussions," she said, not realizing how hard good computer chat was to come by.

5. _____

6. _____

_____

Circle the style technique used in each passage.

It was a crispy, crackly morning. I hurried across the campus kicking the dried, golden yellow and red leaves.

1. **A** short sentences
   B long sentences
   C description
   D dialogue

Here I am in New York. I'm doing fine. I earn a hundred a week. I do all kinds of work. I work very hard. I play very hard. What more could I want? Life is good.

2. **F** dialogue
   G interruptions
   H action
   J short sentences

The original ice creams, like the best homemade varieties today, contained only cream, sugar, flavorings, and occasionally eggs. The prime ingredient was and still is cream, and the kind of cream determines the richness of the final product.

3. **A** dialogue
   B action
   C long sentences
   D short sentences

Dogs' noses—which come in all shapes, sizes, and colors—are a mystery. How do they work so well? Scientists don't know (although they have certainly tried to find out). A person's sense of smell—by comparison—is very limited. All we can do is marvel (and we do) at the dog's ability to find things with its nose.

4. **F** dialogue
   G interruptions
   H short sentences
   J description

I saw Shana (with Keesha in tow) ahead of me on the hill. They always went to school very early—sometimes so early that they had to stand outside waiting for the janitor to open the door.

5. **A** short sentences
   B dialogue
   C interruptions
   D action

Every year about mid-October, the Adams River becomes a frothing maelstrom of flashing, jumping, twisting red sockeye as thousands of salmon arrive to spawn and die.

6. **F** short sentences
   G dialogue
   H interruptions
   J action

Pop sprang to his feet. "What is it?" he asked. "What has frightened you?"
   "It was a wolf, Pop," Sarah gulped, catching her breath. "A great, big wolf!"
   "Where is this wolf now?" Pop shouted.
   "I don't know. It ran into the woods," Sarah replied.

7. **A** description
   B dialogue
   C long sentences
   D action

Identifying Genre

The term **genre** refers to a type or kind of literature. There are four major genres: *fiction*, *nonfiction*, *poetry*, and *drama.*

Fiction is made up. Although it may seem real or even have real people as characters, it is still made up. Some kinds of fiction include science fiction, realistic fiction, historical fiction, myths, and tall tales.

Nonfiction is literature designed to communicate information. Biographies, newspaper and magazine articles, and reports are types of nonfiction.

Poetry paints pictures of ideas or images, using carefully chosen words and sounds. A poem may or may not rhyme. It may be long or short. It may create one image or many images. It may also be a song.

Drama is meant to be performed by actors. When the play is presented, the actors speak and act as characters.

Write *fiction, nonfiction, poetry,* or *drama* to show what genre of literature each description represents.

1. _____   a newspaper editorial

2. _____   a one-act play

3. _____   a script for a television situation comedy

4. _____   the latest best-selling novel

5. _____   a recipe for meatloaf

6. _____   a textbook on grammar and writing

7. _____   nursery rhymes

8. _____   a book of tales about Paul Bunyan

9. _____   the words to a popular song

10. _____   a Broadway play

11. _____   a book of fairy tales

12. _____   a short verse in a greeting card

Write *fiction, nonfiction, poetry,* or *drama* to show what genre of literature each person saw or read.

I am writing this letter to the editor to complain about the biased article written against Senator Fitzwater and published in this newspaper.

1. _____

Last night's performances by the actors of the Little Theater Company of this city leave much to be desired.

2. _____

My friend sent me the most wonderful gift and card. I never realized, until I read her card, how many words rhymed with *birthday.*

3. _____

It is clear why Susan Prince's new novel is such a hit. Its spine-tingling plot twists had this reader guessing until the end as to whodunit.

4. _____

Nina Faber not only is the best cookie maker in the world, but her new cookbook will make you one, too. Try the mint chip cookies. The recipe is easy. The results are delicious.

5. _____

After listening to the Darling Boys perform on their latest hit single, I have to wonder why anyone bothers with this group. Their lyrics are full of rhyme and rhythm signifying nothing.

6. _____

After Mr. Walsh read a series of modern fables to the class, he asked his students to try writing one of their own.

7. _____

After reviewing the list of props and scenery that would be needed and reading the difficult dialects the cast would have to master, the committee decided to look for an alternative play to produce.

8. _____

General Stowe was one of the great military leaders of the last decade. His revealing autobiography is well worth the time.

9. _____

Beautiful, yet simple drawings enhance the beauty of these haiku. Hobbs, the editor of this collection of Japanese verse, has spent many years locating and translating these beautiful word pictures.

10. _____

 **Apply**

Read the information. Then follow the directions.

A volunteer library aide was given a stack of books to put back on the shelves in the library. The aide used the title and the information on the back cover of each book to determine where each book should be shelved.

Read the title, author, and brief description. Then write *fiction, nonfiction, poetry,* or *drama* to show where the aide should place each book.

The Story of My Life by Helen Keller. The interesting biography of this famous woman and the challenges she had to overcome.

1. _____

Romeo and Juliet by William Shakespeare. The famous play about two star-crossed lovers.

2. _____

A Book of Americans by Rosemary and Stephen Vincent Benét. The lives of great American heroes put to verse in this patriotic collection.

3. _____

Chicago Poems by Carl Sandburg. A collection of some of Sandburg's best-known works, including "Fog."

4. _____

Aesop's Fables by Aesop. An illustrated collection of the works of this Greek storyteller.

5. _____

Centennial by James Michener. A saga of the shaping of the West as told through the stories of the characters that populate the created town of Centennial, Colorado.

6. _____

Our Town by Thornton Wilder. One of America's great playwrights shows how special everyday life is.

7. _____

My Life with the Chimpanzees by Jane Goodall. The exciting account of the exploits of one of the world's most celebrated naturalists.

8. _____

◆ D Check Up

Classify each example of literature found in the box by writing it under the correct genre.

movie script	best-selling novel
editorial	Shakespeare's plays
Greek myths	song lyrics
rhyming verse	short story
travel brochure	science report
magazine article	TV drama script
autobiography	advertising jingle
Aesop's fables	science-fiction story
comedy script	haiku
school pageant	greeting-card verse

Fiction

1. _____

2. _____

3. _____

4. _____

5. _____

Poetry

11. _____

12. _____

13. _____

14. _____

15. _____

Nonfiction

6. _____

7. _____

8. _____

9. _____

10. _____

Drama

16. _____

17. _____

18. _____

19. _____

20. _____

A ⟩ Introduce

Applying Passage Elements

Sometimes a reader has to go beyond what has been read and apply what has been gained from the reading. This is sometimes called critical thinking or critical reading.

To **apply** what you have learned, think about what you have read. Go back and reread if necessary. Then, using what you have read and what you know from personal knowledge or experience, apply it to new situations.

Read each passage. Then circle the answer for each question.

Of all sports, basketball is one game that can be traced back to its beginning. In the winter of 1891–92, Dr. James Naismith, a YMCA instructor, invented the game of basketball. He nailed peach baskets to the walls at opposite ends of a gym. Then he set up teams to play this new game. The object of the sport was to toss a soccer ball into one basket. Because Dr. Naismith had 18 players when he invented the game, the first rule was: There shall be 9 players on each side. A short time later, the 5-player rule was adopted.

1. Why do you think the five-player rule was adopted?

   A Some people left the YMCA, so fewer players were available.

   B Naismith decided more teams with fewer players would be better.

   C Nine players per team were too many for the game.

   D Fewer people were interested in playing the game.

Somewhere out in the ocean a blue whale is swimming. It is a great mass of moving blubber. It is the mightiest animal that has ever lived. Its mouth is so big that it can hold a small table and chairs. Yet this giant beast with the giant mouth hasn't any teeth. Instead, it has hundreds of thin plates in its mouth. Its throat is so small that nothing larger than an orange can get through.

It is lucky for such a toothless creature that there is plankton in the water. Plankton is the rich, thick "soup" of the sea; and it is the blue whale's food. It floats near the surface of the water and drifts with the currents. Plankton is made up of the tiniest plants and animals in the sea. The blue whale swims with its mouth open. That way the whale can filter out plankton from the water.

2. What ironic comparison can be made about a whale and its food?

   F The whale's toothless condition allows it to fall prey to smaller animals.

   G The largest creature on earth eats the tiniest plants and animals as its food.

   H A blue whale's small throat prevents it from growing larger.

   J Blue whales and plankton thrive on each other's presence in the ocean waters.

B Practice

Read each passage. Then circle the answer for each question.

The old saying "Feed a cold, starve a fever" goes too far in either case. The best way to treat a cold is to make the sufferer as comfortable as possible. Light, appealing, and easily digested foods make sense for either a cold or a mild fever. And, as most people know, the most important thing to do is drink a lot of fluids. The body's higher temperature during a cold or a fever causes it to lose a lot of water.

1. Based on the passage, what advice is best followed for a cold or a fever?

   A Stay warm but not hot.

   B Stay away from other people who are not sick.

   C Eat what you want, and drink lots of liquids.

   D Wash your hands often and use paper tissues.

Fulton's Folly sounds like the name of a Broadway stage show, but it was actually the name of a steamship. The "Folly" got its nickname from the many people who believed that Robert Fulton, the inventor of the steamship, had made a big mistake, or folly, in trying to build a ship that ran on steam power. When the day of the ship's launching arrived, crowds lined the shore to watch it set out on its first voyage. Despite the doubts of the skeptics, Fulton's Folly made a splendid trip. After the successful voyage, many more steamboats were built.

2. Why would inventors want to find a new way to power ships?

   F Inventors are strange people.

   G Sailing was old-fashioned.

   H Few people knew how to operate sails any longer.

   J People wanted faster, more dependable ways of making ships move.

Many forces have been at work for a long time changing the face of the land upon which we live. These forces are the weather, water, and living things. If it were not for these forces, the land would be nothing but solid rock. It would not be able to support life. The work of all these forces on the earth's surface is called erosion. Of all these forces, however, running water has done the most to change the surface of the land.

3. What is an example of running water causing erosion and changing the surface of the land?

   A A broken water pipe floods a basement.

   B Rainwater creates a small channel in a gravel driveway.

   C Flooding carries a house off its foundation.

   D Melting snow forms puddles of water.

C ▶ Apply

Read the passages. Then answer the questions.

Have you ever heard of farms for wild animals? The University of Alaska has one. It's an experimental farm that raises musk oxen. At one time, the oxen were dying out, and few of the animals were left. Now because of the work going on at the farm, the musk oxen have not only been saved but also been put to work.

1. What other animals might make good candidates for wild animal farms? Why?

_____

_____

_____

Many people have never heard of Chester Greenwood. Yet, the invention for which he is best known has been in common use for many years. Greenwood invented earmuffs. He also invented a few other things, including the springtooth rake, airplane shock absorbers, and self-priming spark plugs. But most of those who remember him remember him only as the inventor of earmuffs.

2. Why do you think Chester Greenwood is best remembered for inventing earmuffs?

_____

_____

_____

How would you like a nice dish of animal bones for dessert? Most people would prefer something more appealing, like gelatin, for example. What they don't realize is that gelatin is a protein substance that comes from the skin and bones of animals. Making gelatin is a complicated process. When the process is complete, the gelatin is concentrated, chilled, sliced, and dried. Dried gelatin is sold in the form of sheets, flakes, or powder. Then it is ready to make a tasty dessert.

3. Why might people prefer not to know where their gelatin salads and desserts come from?

_____

_____

_____

Read each passage. Then circle the answer for each question.

Arctic tundra is found in the far north near the Arctic Ocean. It is a flat, treeless area covered by mosses, lichens, grasses, and small shrubs. Tundra often looks like a gray-green plain with many lakes and ponds. In the fall the tundra's colors change to red and brown.

An important part of the Arctic tundra is the permafrost layer. This is a layer of frozen water and soil that remains protected all year beneath the top layer of soil and plants. Permafrost prevents water from draining away.

The warm season in the tundra is very short, so the tiny plants can only grow a little bit each year.

1. With what might the plants of the tundra be compared?

   A the lush assortment of green plants in a rain forest

   B the blanket of snow and ice covering the continent of Antarctica

   C trees in other parts of the world that change colors when the seasons change

   D other annuals that are planted for a summer display of color

Very hot and very cold foods can change your sense of taste. Heat increases your ability to taste. You can taste very small amounts of sugar in hot coffee. But a lot more sugar is needed to make ice cream and other cold foods taste sweet.

Your sense of smell is another thing that can change your sense of taste. You can prove this by drinking chocolate while holding your nose. You'll find that it doesn't taste much like chocolate. If you really want a surprise, hold your nose and close your eyes while somebody gives you a bite of onion and a bite of apple. You won't be able to taste the difference.

2. Who might be interested in investigating this information further?

   F doctors who specialize in the mouth

   G scientists studying nerves

   H nutritionists who specialize in healthy diets

   J companies developing new food packaging

The Chinese willow leaf pattern is an old and popular design for dishes. But at one time a person who owned one of these dishes could have been charged with treason. In the 15th century, Chinese secret societies drew symbols and emblems on the plates to transmit messages. The Manchu rulers of China wanted to prevent those societies from gathering too much power. So they outlawed the making and use of willow pattern dishes. Anyone who was caught owning or using the plates could be arrested.

3. Why do you think dishes were used in this way?

   A Secret society members were also dish makers.

   B Symbols could easily be hidden in the willow branches.

   C When houses were searched, dishes were ignored.

   D The dishes were common items that could quickly be broken or destroyed.

Read On   Read "A Matter of Taste." Use the skills developed in Lessons 10–12 to answer the questions.

Predicting Outcomes

A story's outcome can often be predicted by using what you have read and what you already know.

Identifying Fact and Opinion

Facts are statements that can be proved. Opinions are ideas, beliefs, or judgments—statements that cannot be proved.

Recognizing Author's Purpose

The most common purposes for writing are to entertain, to inform, to persuade or express an opinion, to describe, and to explain or instruct.

Recognizing Author's Point of View

An author's point of view is how he or she feels about the characters or topics. An author's point of view may be positive or negative.

Making Generalizations

A generalization is a conclusion that applies to many people, facts, events, or situations. Generalizations are conclusions based on facts or specific examples.

Identifying Style Techniques

Authors use specific words, types of sentences, and different kinds of organization to create a certain feel. The style helps extend the meaning of the written work.

Identifying Genre

Genre refers to a type or kind of literature such as fiction, poetry, drama, or nonfiction.

Applying Passage Elements

Sometimes you must go beyond what you have read and apply it to help you understand certain elements in a passage.

Assessment

Read the paragraphs and circle the answer for each question.

Garrett A. Morgan was the inventor of the gas mask. The mask was an airtight canvas hood that was worn over the head. The hood was connected to a special breathing tube that hung to the ground. Before people would use Morgan's invention, he had to prove that it would work. Morgan had a man wearing the mask go into a small, smoke-filled tent. He stayed there for 20 minutes. Then he went into a room filled with poison gas and stayed there for 15 minutes. Firefighters then used the masks to save people trapped in a subway tunnel. Morgan's invention finally won acceptance when Morgan and his brother wore the masks to save more than 20 workers who were trapped in a smoke-filled water tunnel below Lake Erie.

1. What generalization can you make from this paragraph?

   A People will not accept new inventions until it is proved that they work.

   B An inventor's word is all that is necessary for a new invention to be accepted.

   C The gas mask was an invention that had few practical applications.

   D Good publicity made gas masks a success.

2. What is the author's purpose?

   F to explain how a gas mask works

   G to persuade people to purchase gas masks

   H to tell readers about the invention of the gas mask and how it came to be accepted

   J to convince people that Garrett Morgan was a great inventor

Samuel Langhorne Clemens was raised in Hannibal, Missouri, a village on the Mississippi River. There he was able to observe steamboat life, gamblers, swindlers, slave dealers, and other river travelers. Instead of attending high school and college, Clemens gained his education as a printer, newspaper reporter, and riverboat pilot. He based many of his short stories, sketches, essays, narratives, and novels on his personal experiences. Have you read *The Adventures of Tom Sawyer, The Prince and the Pauper,* or *A Connecticut Yankee in King Arthur's Court?* Then you are familiar with the works of Samuel Clemens, who is better known as Mark Twain. Twain may be the greatest humorist in American literature.

3. Which sentence is *not* a fact?

   A Samuel Langhorne Clemens was raised in Hannibal, Missouri.

   B Clemens gained his education as a printer, newspaper reporter, and riverboat pilot.

   C Samuel Clemens is better known as Mark Twain.

   D Twain may be the greatest humorist in American literature.

4. Mark Twain is

   F the name of Samuel Clemens's friend

   G the name of Samuel Clemens's father

   H the name Samuel Clemens wrote under

   J the name of a book written by Samuel Clemens

Would you believe that part of your body is as strong as steel? It's your bones. A cubic inch of human bone can take four thousand pounds of pressure without breaking. That makes it about as strong as steel. Bone is made of two major substances—calcium and collagen. Calcium is a mineral. It makes bones hard. Collagen is a protein. Scientists say that collagen helps bones withstand impact without breaking. Bones can flex slightly, rather than break, when hit.

5. Collagen makes bones

   A hard

   B breakable

   C like steel

   D flexible

6. This paragraph would most likely be found in a

   F novel

   G government report

   H textbook

   J play

If there's one rule you should remember if you're ever stranded in the middle of the ocean, it's don't drink the water. It can be fatal to drink ocean water. Ocean water is too salty for humans to drink. An average gallon of ocean water contains nearly a quarter pound of salt. The human body requires salt in very small amounts. Someone who drank a quart of salt water would quickly become dehydrated.

7. Salt causes the body to become

   A expanded

   B dehydrated

   C tired

   D refreshed

8. From this paragraph you can generalize that all people who drink a quart of salt water would

   F no longer be thirsty

   G die faster from salt poisoning than from thirst

   H have extra energy

   J learn to like salty water.

9. What is the author's purpose?

   A to entertain readers with a scary story

   B to describe the composition of ocean water

   C to explain why people should not drink salt water

   D to tell why the human body needs small amounts of salt

(1) Sadly, old-fashioned country inns have just about completely given way to modern hotels and motels. (2) Only a couple of hundred years ago, the first inns were private homes where people would gladly give food and shelter in exchange for company and stories from the outside world. (3) It was the revolution in transportation—the advent of the train, the automobile, and the airplane—that brought about huge impersonal resorts. (4) And it was the highway that led to the motel, which is short for motor hotel. (5) Motels are usually located right next to noisy interstate highways. (6) There is no hospitality in such places, but motels do offer inexpensive lodging.

10. Which style technique does the author use?

   F dialogue

   G short, choppy sentences

   H descriptive details

   J scientific examples

11. The author seems to be

   A careful not to take sides

   B unhappy that modern impersonal lodging has replaced old-fashioned hospitality

   C glad that inexpensive lodging is available

   D glad that motels make it easy for people to travel

12. Which sentence contains both a fact *and* an opinion?

   F sentence 1

   G sentence 2

   H sentence 4

   J sentence 6

Posttest

Circle the word that is spelled correctly and best completes each sentence.

1. My dentist discovered three _____ during my annual check-up.

   A cavityies

   B cavitees

   C cavities

   D caviteies

2. That package is much _____ than this one.

   F heavier

   G heavyier

   H heaver

   J heavyer

3. We placed a holiday _____ on our front door.

   A reathe

   B wreath

   C wreeth

   D wreate

4. Cathy _____ vote because she didn't register in time.

   F couldn't

   G culn't

   H couldnt

   J coudn't

Circle the answer that is a synonym for the underlined word.

5. relate the story

   A tell

   B forget

   C embellish

   D reinforce

6. advance in medicine

   F retreat

   G disinterest

   H decline

   J progress

7. profess his loyalty

   A dispute

   B deny

   C declare

   D displace

8. emblem of peace

   F idea

   G song

   H symbol

   J motto

9. excellent rating

   A mediocre

   B superior

   C bad

   D unfair

10. blunt instrument

   F sharp

   G shiny

   H dull

   J dangerous

Circle the answer that is an antonym for the underlined word.

11. frown on her face
    A grimace
    B smile
    C smirk
    D wrinkle

12. gather the leaves
    F scatter
    G collect
    H rake
    J bury

13. fond greeting
    A wishes
    B farewell
    C introduction
    D welcome

14. gush of warm water
    F stream
    G shower
    H flow
    J trickle

15. honest businessman
    A truthful
    B opinionated
    C deceitful
    D successful

16. liberal politician
    F disarming
    G conservative
    H popular
    J famous

Circle the answer for each question.

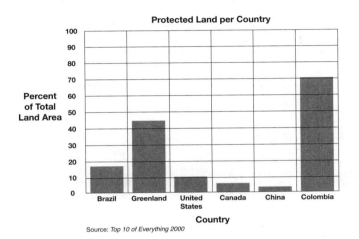

Protected Land per Country

Source: *Top 10 of Everything 2000*

17. Which country has the greatest amount of protected land?

   A Greenland

   B Colombia

   C United States

   D Brazil

18. About how much more protected land does Greenland have than the United States?

   F 35%

   G 25%

   H 10%

   J 5%

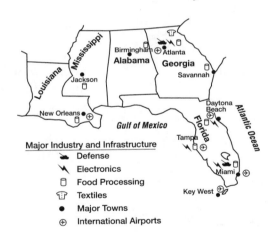

Major Industry and Infrastructure
- 🛬 Defense
- ⋏ Electronics
- ▯ Food Processing
- 👕 Textiles
- ● Major Towns
- ⊕ International Airports

19. What is the major industry in Savannah, Georgia?

   A electronics

   B textiles

   C food processing

   D defense

20. Which state does *not* have an international airport?

   F Georgia

   G Florida

   H Louisiana

   J Mississippi

21. If the guide words on a dictionary page are *order* and *organ,* which word would be found on the page?

    A ore

    B organize

    C origin

    D orchid

22. Which words are *not* in alphabetical order?

    F misery, misled, misprint, mismatch

    G negotiate, neighbor, neither, nephew

    H skeptical, skin, skirt, sky

    J track, trail, train, trash

Index

Chile

    ancestry, 26
    government
        armed forces, 38
        courts, 40
        local, 41
        national, 44–45
    land,
        Archipelago, 50
        Central Valley, 52
        Northern Desert, 53
    language, 55
    people, 54–62

23. Which word matches this pronunciation? (hüz)

    A hose

    B house

    C whose

    D huts

24. Under what entry will you find information about education and recreation in Chile?

    F ancestry

    G land

    H language

    J people

25. Where would you add an entry for "history"?

    A between government and land

    B between land and language

    C between ancestry and government

    D after people

26. What information would you expect to be asked on *both* a license application and a mail-order form?

    F DOB

    G address

    H number of items

    J shipping and handling fee

27. When ordering through a catalog, a consumer should provide all of the following information except

   A credit card number

   B quantity of items ordered

   C social security number

   D total amount of order

28. A person seeking a part-time job would look for which of the following abbreviations in a want ad?

   F P.O.

   G P/T

   H EOE

   J Exp.

29. What information is *not* included on a resumé?

   A credit card number

   B education

   C work experience

   D applicant's phone number

There were over 1500 people on the cruise ship, all intending to have a good time. It happened on the third night at sea during the captain's gala. First the waiters began to have trouble balancing their trays full of dishes. Then waves started to wash over the main deck. Soon the ship began to tilt dangerously as the captain radioed for help. Passenger Jill Wilson later recalled, "All I remember is water rising and almost knocking me over. When the emergency warning sounded, I left my cabin and started toward the life boat station. Then I saw those children at the end of the hall. I knew I couldn't leave them. I waded into the hall. It wasn't easy because the ship was rocking. But somehow I got to them."

30. The word that best describes Jill Wilson is

   F selfish

   G strong

   H courageous

   J intelligence

31. What was the first sign that the ship was in trouble?

   A The ship began to tilt.

   B Waves washed over the main deck.

   C The waiters had trouble balancing their trays.

   D Water filled the ship's hallways.

Posttest *continued*

You've probably heard the expression *sly as a fox*. But how did the fox get its reputation for being a clever animal? Probably from fox hunters. A hunter tries to catch a fox by chasing after it on a horse. The hunter sends a pack of hound dogs ahead to find the fox. The dogs pick up the fox's scent and chase it down. Rather than slipping into the nearest thicket, the fox may keep on running just to keep the chase alive. Though a fox can run as fast as 25 miles per hour, it is not as fast as a hound. And if it ever had to fight a hound, the fox, which weighs only around ten pounds, would be in big trouble. By crossing streams, running along the tops of fences and darting through the woods, a fox can keep a pack of hounds totally confused.

32. From this paragraph you can conclude that a fox survives a hunt by

    F   using its brain

    G   being stronger than the hounds

    H   running faster than the hounds

    J   hiding in the forest

33. Which sentence supports the idea that the fox enjoys a good chase as much as the hounds do?

    A   Though a fox can run as fast as 25 miles per hour, it is not as fast as a hound.

    B   By crossing streams, running along the tops of fences and darting through the woods, a fox can keep a pack of hounds totally confused.

    C   The dogs pick up the fox's scent and chase it down.

    D   Rather than slipping into the nearest thicket, the fox may keep on running just to keep the chase alive.

34. To tell the reader about the fox's cleverness, the author

    F   explains how the hunters try to capture foxes

    G   tells a story about an actual fox hunt

    H   uses examples of clever things a fox does

    J   describes the animal's size

Anyone with even a passing interest in our city's history should join the protest against the construction of high-rise apartment buildings in the downtown area. This unnecessary housing project would replace a row of historic shops that date from the turn of the century and that are the backbone of the downtown shopping area. The housing plan, which makes no provision for parking or pedestrian traffic, seems to have been created with only one thing in mind: to line the pockets of wealthy developers who have no vested interest in our community. All who consider themselves good citizens of Oak Creek should actively work to block the construction of these apartments.

35. What is the author's purpose in this paragraph?

    A   to convince the reader that additional housing is needed in the downtown area

    B   to inform the reader about downtown development

    C   to explain how to build high-rise apartments

    D   to persuade the reader to join in the protest against the downtown apartment project

242

36. Based on the paragraph, what do you think the author might do?

    F move to a new community

    G campaign for a candidate who is in favor of preserving the historic downtown area

    H follow the progress of the apartment project by reading the daily newspaper

    J purchase an apartment when the project is complete

37. Where might you read this selection?

    A on the editorial page of a newspaper

    B in a personal journal

    C in a book of poetry

    D in a science textbook

38. Which phrase expresses the author's opinion?

    F no provision for parking

    G unnecessary housing project

    H row of historic houses

    J high-rise apartment buildings

A cat's whiskers are very important. They are extremely sensitive sense organs. They help the cat judge the width of tight spaces before trying to squeeze through. Whiskers also work like weather vanes. They tell the cat which way the wind is blowing. More importantly, the stimulation of a cat's whiskers triggers a blinking reflex. For instance, if a jutting twig or other hazard touches the whiskers, the cat blinks its eyes to protect them from damage. If you have a cat, you can see this reflex by lightly brushing the cat's whiskers.

39. What generalization can you make from this paragraph?

    A All cats use their whiskers to communicate.

    B Every cat's whiskers extend the animal's sense of touch.

    C Every cat's whiskers make up for deficiencies in its vision.

    D On all cats, whiskers grow on the chin, at the sides of the face, and above the eyes.

40. The author compares a cat's whiskers to a

    F blinking eye

    G weather vane

    H cane

    J hearing aid

41. What is the main idea of this paragraph?

    A Cats have quick reflexes.

    B Cats can fit in small places if they rely on their whiskers.

    C Cats are not the only animals who have whiskers.

    D A cat's whiskers are special hairs that serve as highly sensitive touch organs.

Posttest Answer Key and Evaluation Chart

This posttest has been designed to check your mastery of the reading skills studied. Circle the question numbers that you answered incorrectly and review the practice pages covering those skills. Carefully rework those practice pages to be sure you understand those skills.

Key

1.	C
2.	F
3.	B
4.	F
5.	A
6.	J
7.	C
8.	H
9.	B
10.	H
11.	B
12.	F
13.	B
14.	J
15.	C
16.	G
17.	B
18.	F
19.	C
20.	J
21.	A
22.	F
23.	C
24.	J
25.	A
26.	G
27.	C
28.	G
29.	A
30.	H
31.	C
32.	F
33.	D
34.	H
35.	D
36.	G
37.	A
38.	G
39.	B
40.	G

Tested Skills	Question Numbers	Practice Pages
Synonyms	5–10	21–24, 25–28
Antonyms	11–16	29–32, 33–36
Context clues		37–40, 41–44
Spelling	1–4	45–48, 49–52
Details		59–62, 63–66
Sequence	31	67–70, 71–74
Stated concepts		75–78, 79–82
Graphs	17, 18	89–92
Maps	19, 20	93–96
Dictionary	21–23	97–100
Index	24, 25	101–104
Reference sources		105–108
Library catalog card		105–108
Forms	26, 27	109–112
Consumer materials	28, 29	113–116, 117–120
Characters	30	127–130, 131–134
Main idea	41	135–138, 139–142
Compare/contrast	40	143–146, 147–150
Drawing conclusions	32	151–154, 155–158
Supporting evidence	33	175–178
Predicting outcomes	36	185–188, 189–192
Identifying fact and opinion	38	193–196, 197–200
Author's purpose	35	201–204, 205–208
Generalizations	39	217–220
Style techniques	34	221–224
Genre	37	225–228

Answer Key

◆ Unit 1 Words in Context

Page 19: 1. microwave; electromagnetic wave with a wavelength between one millimeter and 30 centimeters, **2.** microscope; device with lens for making small things look larger, **3.** astronomer; person who studies the moon, planets, and stars, **4.** asterisk; star-shaped mark, **5.** inscribe; write words on stone, metal, or paper, **6.** scribble; write carelessly or hastily, **7.** spectacle; something to look at, **8.** inspector; someone whose job it is to examine something

Page 20: 1. stopped for a while, **2.** hung by fastening to something above, **3.** piece of stone, **4.** a kind of popular music with a strong beat and a simple melody, **5.** place where justice is administered, **6.** place marked off for a game, **7.** small room, **8.** basic unit of living matter

◆ Lesson 1 Recognizing Synonyms

Page 21: 1. glad, **2.** uninteresting, **3.** tiny, **4.** silly, **5.** end, **6.** sleepy, **7.** mad, **8.** caring, **9.** shout, **10.** want

Possible answers: **11.** buy, **12.** faster, **13.** night, **14.** easier, **15.** unhappy

Page 22: Possible answers: **1.** happy, nice, glad, **2.** destroy, wreck, break, **3.** large, huge, tall, **4.** wonderful, important, great, **5.** concerned, troubled, upset, **6.** beat, pound, thump, **7.** silly, humorous, amusing, **8.** complete, end, stop, **9.** powerful, tough, mighty, **10.** enjoy, prefer, love

Page 23: 1. additional, **2.** searched, **3.** present, **4.** liked, **5.** funny, **6.** group, **7.** pictures, **8.** purchased, **9.** famous, **10.** writer

Page 24: 1. D, **2.** F, **3.** B, **4.** F, **5.** D, **6.** G, **7.** B, **8.** F

◆ Lesson 2 Using Synonyms

Page 25: 1. performer, **2.** evil, **3.** gathering, **4.** remain, **5.** prison, **6.** jelly, **7.** giving, **8.** understand

Page 26: 1. monster, **2.** think, **3.** swear, **4.** photographs, **5.** fuzzy, **6.** searched, **7.** caught, **8.** sure

Page 27: Possible answers: **1.** huge, **2.** trip, **3.** exhausting, **4.** cheap, **5.** lovely, **6.** crowded, **7.** several, **8.** letter, **9.** enjoyed, **10.** bright, **11.** chilly, **12.** glad, **13.** excited, **14.** nice, **15.** nearby

Page 28: 1. A, **2.** H, **3.** C, **4.** G, **5.** A, **6.** G, **7.** C, **8.** G

◆ Lesson 3 Recognizing Antonyms

Page 29: 1. high, **2.** answer, **3.** after, **4.** last, **5.** catch, **6.** night, **7.** false, **8.** fancy, **9.** far, **10.** stale, **11.** smooth, **12.** cold, **13.** full, **14.** hate, **15.** cry

Page 30: Possible answers: **1.** dirty, **2.** clumsy, **3.** cool, **4.** closed, **5.** talk, **6.** never, **7.** on, **8.** loud, **9.** back, **10.** healthy, **11.** stop, **12.** sour, **13.** tight, **14.** narrow, **15.** tame

Page 31: 1. weak, **2.** dishonest, **3.** subtract, **4.** laugh, **5.** sell, **6.** backward, **7.** fat, **8.** pull

Possible answers: **9.** bad, **10.** strenuous, **11.** long, **12.** slowly, **13.** up

Page 32: 1. B, **2.** F, **3.** D, **4.** G, **5.** D, **6.** F, **7.** C, **8.** G

◆ Lesson 4 Using Antonyms

Page 33: 1. out, **2.** few, **3.** old, **4.** thawed, **5.** asleep, **6.** south, **7.** part, **8.** take, **9.** back, **10.** save, **11.** funny, **12.** difficult, **13.** win, **14.** slow, **15.** after

Page 34: Across: 2. old, **4.** low, **5.** up, **6.** compliment, **8.** give, **10.** less, **11.** right
Down: 1. cool, **2.** open, **3.** close, **7.** insult, **9.** high

Page 35: Possible answers: **1.** dry, **2.** right, **3.** rough, **4.** dishonest, **5.** clear
Sentences will vary.
Possible answers: **6.** colorful, bright, shiny, **7.** mean, cruel, nasty, **8.** hot, oppressive, warm, **9.** sad, unhappy, depressed

Page 36: 1. B, **2.** H, **3.** A, **4.** J, **5.** B, **6.** J, **7.** B, **8.** F

◆ Lesson 5 Recognizing Context Clues

Page 37: Possible meanings: **1.** one-of-a-kind, **2.** different, **3.** ways of living, **4.** newcomers, **5.** busy

Page 38: 1. useful, **2.** use up, **3.** necessary, **4.** make, **5.** people, **6.** let

Page 39: Possible meanings: **1.** make loud sounds, **2.** brave, **3.** disorder, **4.** parties, **5.** soaked, **6.** turned red, **7.** rough, **8.** picture, **9.** dangerous, **10.** foolish

Page 40: 1. B, **2.** H, **3.** D, **4.** F, **5.** C, **6.** F

◆ Lesson 6 Using Context Clues

Page 41: 1. make, **2.** joining, **3.** not able, **4.** the process of breaking down

Answer Key *continued*

Page 42: 1. prickly weeds, **2.** the groupings of plants and animals, **3.** breathing tube, **4.** ready to eat, **5.** introduction to the book, **6.** several tunes one after the other, **7.** tall tower with a bright light, **8.** small, biting flies

Page 43: 1. changed, **2.** copy, **3.** fashion, **4.** fascinating, **5.** made to seem smaller, **6.** pleated strips of cloth, **7.** shoes

Page 44: 1. B, **2.** H, **3.** A, **4.** G, **5.** C, **6.** J

◆ Lesson 7 Spelling Words

Page 45: 1. bats, batches, babies, **2.** branches, bottles, lobbies, **3.** bodies, grasses, beds, **4.** desks, canaries, bushes

Page 46: 1. shape, **2.** thunder, **3.** wheel, **4.** thirsty, **5.** whale, **6.** sheets, **7.** whine, **8.** ships, **9.** whistle, **10.** thirty, **11.** Sharks, **12.** thick

Page 47: 1. scene, **2.** scent, **3.** sign, **4.** wren, **5.** gnome, **6.** wrap, **7.** write, **8.** knock, **9.** knot, **10.** knee

Page 48: 1. A, **2.** G, **3.** C, **4.** G, **5.** B, **6.** F, **7.** B, **8.** H, **9.** A, **10.** H

◆ Lesson 8 Spelling Words

Page 49: 1. biggest, **2.** happier, **3.** heaviest, **4.** campground, **5.** firefly, **6.** can't, **7.** I'm

Page 50: 1. armchair, **2.** strawberry, **3.** newspaper, **4.** everything, **5.** bedroom, **6.** campground, **7.** flashlight, **8.** suitcase, **9.** waterproof, **10.** cupcake

Page 51: 1. I've, **2.** wouldn't, **3.** what's, **4.** it's, **5.** there's, **6.** couldn't, **7.** I'm, **8.** can't, **9.** didn't, **10.** she'd, **11.** there's, **12.** can't, **13.** I'm, **14.** I've, **15.** didn't

Page 52: 1. A, **2.** H, **3.** C, **4.** F, **5.** B, **6.** H, **7.** B, **8.** H, **9.** B, **10.** F

◆ Unit 1 Review

Page 53:
Synonyms: remember
Antonyms: reality
Context Clues: people who move from place to place in search of grazing land for their herds
Spelling Words: cannons, ditches, batteries; wring, knob; thinner, thinnest, heavier, heaviest; baseball; he'll, don't

◆ Unit 1 Assessment

Page 54: 1. B, **2.** F, **3.** B, **4.** H, **5.** A, **6.** J, **7.** C, **8.** J, **9.** B, **10.** F, **11.** D, **12.** F, **13.** C, **14.** F, **15.** D, **16.** H, **17.** C, **18.** H, **19.** A, **20.** H, **21.** D, **22.** G, **23.** C, **24.** J, **25.** B, **26.** F, **27.** B, **28.** J, **29.** A, **30.** J, **31.** C

◆ Unit 2 Recalling Information

Page 57: 1. to guess or understand correctly, **2.** wait, **3.** raining hard, **4.** a better position, advantage, **5.** sick, ailing
Possible answers: **6.** Grandpa is feeling in the pink. **7.** Martha has a green thumb. **8.** The bad news hit me from out of the blue. **9.** Scott sees red when anyone borrows his bike without asking.

Page 58: 1. E, **2.** J, **3.** A, **4.** B, **5.** G, **6.** H, **7.** D, **8.** I, **9.** C, **10.** F

◆ Lesson 1 Identifying Details

Page 59: 1. Scientists have improved popcorn. **2. a.** Better popcorn from Latin America was crossed with American popcorn. **b.** Japanese hull-less popcorn was crossed with American popcorn.

Page 60: 1. stagecoaches mounted on four wheels, **2.** eight, **3.** wood stoves, **4.** candles in sconces nailed to the walls, **5.** made the ride smoother, **6.** drew out the smoke, **7.** lamps, **8.** electric lights

Page 61: 1. explain a fact or an idea, **2.** one percent of the body's weight in water is lost, **3.** a message is sent to glands in your mouth, **4. a.** It carries food to cells. **b.** It removes wastes from cells. **c.** It keeps the body at the right temperature.

Page 62: 1. A, **2.** G, **3.** D, **4.** G, **5.** C, **6.** G

◆ Lesson 2 Recognizing Details

Page 63: 1. A, **2.** B, **3.** B, **4.** C, **5.** A rat may eat one-third of its own weight in 24 hours.

Page 64: 1. A, **2.** B, **3.** C, **4.** A, **5.** He hit 15 home runs and drove in 50 runs.

Page 65: 1. A, **2. a.** Native Americans used green leaves on wounds. **b.** They used mint tea for cramps. **c.** They used wintergreen leaves for massages. **3.** B, **4.** She carried a big briefcase. Long hair was pulled back. Her voice was strong and powerful.

Page 66: 1. C, **2.** J, **3.** A, **4.** G, **5.** B, **6.** G

Answer Key *continued*

◆ Lesson 3 Identifying Sequence

Page 67: 1. Douglas Corrigan left New York.
2. a day later, **3.** Later, **4.** from that time until now

Page 68: 6, 2, 5, 1, 3, 4
in 1841, Eighteen months later, Finally, By 1847,
In 1861, After the war

Page 69: 1. 13, **2.** 1911, **3.** stop signs, **4.** 35 miles
per hour, **5.** 55 miles per hour, **6.** electric cars

Page 70: 1. B, **2.** G, **3.** A, **4.** H, **5.** C, **6.** J

◆ Lesson 4 Recognizing Sequence

Page 71: 1. Find a salad bowl to use. **2.** Wash
and shred the lettuce. **3.** Put the lettuce in a
salad bowl. **4.** Top with carrots. **5.** Slice eggs,
tomatoes, and cucumbers. **6.** Put them around
the side of the bowl. **7.** Put chicken in the
middle. **8.** Top with cheese.

Page 72: 1. Fog in London turned deadly.
2. Fog was formed in cool air trapped under
a layer of warm air. **3.** Pollutants came from
furnaces. **4.** London was covered by a black fog.
5. Thousands of people died.

Page 73: Step 1
Keep the dog in one room.
Check on your dog periodically.
Step 2
After three good days, let it in another room.
Step 3
Let the dog be alone for short periods of time.
Step 4
Let the dog be in more rooms for longer periods
of time.

Page 74: 1. Cold air cools the water on the
surface. **2.** It is heavier than warm water.
3. Warm water rises to the top. **4.** until the water
temperature is 39 degrees, **5.** The water becomes
lighter as it gets colder. **6.** when the surface
temperature is 32 degrees

◆ Lesson 5 Stated Concepts

Page 75: 1. A, **2.** B, **3.** B, **4.** C

Page 76: 1. four, **2.** five tons, **3.** not stated, **4.** six,
5. He worked to develop a fire engine and pay
firefighters. **6.** not stated, **7.** German Alps, **8.** five
hundred feet, **9.** not stated, **10.** not stated

Page 77: 1. (2), **2.** (6), **3.** (3), **4.** (4), **5.** (1), **6.** (4), **7.** (6)

Page 78: 1. B, **2.** H, **3.** A, **4.** J, **5.** D, **6.** G

◆ Lesson 6 Understanding Stated Concepts

Page 79: 1. sand fleas, **2.** They leap into the air
like fleas. They live in sand. **3.** Sand fleas and
fleas both leap into the air. **4.** Sand fleas don't
bite like fleas. Sand fleas are not insects. They
are crustaceans. **5.** They live under masses of
tangled seaweed high on beaches. **6.** No, the
passage states that they live in a colony, which
is a group of animals that live together.

Page 80: 1. false; It is a way of changing the
ocean's heat into energy. **2.** true, **3.** true, **4.** false;
It was built in Cuba. **5.** false; It was not
successful. **6.** true

Page 81: 1. one of the largest mountains in the
solar system, **2.** 1.2 miles higher than Mount
Everest, **3.** 35,300 feet above Venus's plain level,
4. a very rocky surface, **5.** a volcanic crater

Page 82: 1. B, **2.** H, **3.** D, **4.** G, **5.** A, **6.** F

◆ Unit 2 Assessment

Page 84: 1. B, **2.** H, **3.** C, **4.** J, **5.** C, **6.** H, **7.** D,
8. H, **9.** A, **10.** H, **11.** D, **12.** H

◆ Unit 3 Graphic Information

Page 87: 1. E, **2.** H, **3.** I, **4.** G, **5.** B, **6.** A, **7.** J, **8.** F,
9. C, **10.** D

Page 88: Possible answers: **1.** persistent;
Sentences will vary. **2.** sneaky; Sentences will
vary. **3.** path; Sentences will vary. **4.** scale;
Sentences will vary. **5.** crush; Sentences will vary.
6. pretty; Sentences will vary. **7.** gem; Sentences
will vary. **8.** soothing; Sentences will vary.

◆ Lesson 1 Using Graphs

Page 89: 1. managers, **2.** service, **3.**
technical/sales, **4.** about $250, **5.** about $125

Page 90: 1. 12:00, **2.** 2:00 and 3:00, **3.** 11:00,
4. 2:00 and 3:00, **5.** 50

Page 91: 1. 24%, **2.** 8%, **3.** natural gas, **4.** other,
5. petroleum

Page 92: 1. B, **2.** G, **3.** C, **4.** G, **5.** D

◆ Lesson 2 Reading Maps

Page 93: 1. the intersection of C Street and Third
Avenue, **2.** one block, **3.** Front Street, **4.** C Street,
5. First Street

Answer Key *continued*

Page 94: 1. city hall, **2.** school, **3.** library, **4.** aquarium, **5.** hospital, **6.** D7, **7.** A6, **8.** C1

Page 95: 1. 6, **2.** 20 miles, **3.** northwest, **4.** 14, **5.** C1

Page 96: 1. B, **2.** H, **3.** C, **4.** G, **5.** A

◆ Lesson 3 Using the Dictionary

Page 97: 1. ant, elephant, horse, **2.** paper, pencil, pepper, **3.** cellar, cellophane, cello, Celtic, **4.** lapel, lapse, larch, lapdog, **5.** convent, convention, convene, convenient

Page 98: 1–5 Answers will vary depending on dictionary used. Possible answers: **1.** (büt), **2.** (hėrd), **3.** (strĭk), **4.** (krôl), **5.** (klən), **6.** bomb, **7.** cashier, **8.** crook, **9.** evade, **10.** haze, **11.** bail, **12.** laugh, **13.** measure, **14.** giraffe, **15.** jewel

Page 99: 1. 2, **2.** 1, **3.** 4, **4.** 3, **5.** 1, **6.** 2, **7.** 2, **8.** 4, **9.** 1

Page 100: 1. C, **2.** H, **3.** B, **4.** G, **5.** A, **6.** H, **7.** D

◆ Lesson 4 Using Indexes

Page 101: 1. 164, **2.** Babysitters and Children's Activities, **3.** Camping under Accommodations, Campgrounds, **4.** Boat Tours, **5.** Airport, Air Travel

Page 102: 1. true, **2.** false; The picture is on page 220. **3.** true, **4.** false; There is no picture on page 95. **5.** false; It is a plant.

Page 103: 1. 3, **2.** Salmon with Dill, **3.** 37, **4.** no, **5.** 2, **6.** Spicy Chicken Salad, **7.** 34, **8.** yes, Pepper and Tomato Salad, Tomato with Cheese, **9.** in alphabetical order

Page 104: 1. B, **2.** G, **3.** C, **4.** F, **5.** C, **6.** J

◆ Lesson 5 Using Reference Sources

Page 105: 1. Shaping Up: Exercises for Water Sports, **2.** 252, **3.** ill, **4.** Healthy Living Books, **5.** physical fitness, exercise, aquatic sports, **6.** The number tells you where to find the book in the library.

Page 106: 1. weather, **2.** blizzard, **3.** cloud, **4.** barometer, **5.** hurricane

Page 107: 1. daily or weekly, **2.** news, articles, ads, and opinions, **3.** *National Newspaper Index*, **4.** Possible answers: *The New York Times, The Christian Science Monitor, The Wall Street Journal, Los Angeles Times, Washington Post*, **5.** No, the index lists only articles from the last three years; a 1990 article would be too old.

6. *Readers' Guide to Periodical Literature*, **7.** Possible answers: They come out on a regular basis. They contain news, articles, ads, and opinions. Their articles are listed in indexes that can be used as reference sources.

Page 108: 1. B, **2.** G, **3.** D, **4.** F, **5.** C, **6.** H, **7.** B

◆ Lesson 6 Forms

Page 109: 1. No; The directions say not to write above the line. **2.** student, **3.** to show that the applicant is responsible, **4.** Answers will vary.

Page 110: Check form. **1.** date of birth, **2.** no, **3.** Possible answer: to verify that the dog has had proper shots and care, **4.** Possible answer: so authorities can identify the dog for whom the license is intended

Page 111: Check form. **1.** $25.90, **2.** Answers will vary. **3.** Add the two amounts and delivery. **4.** Possible answer: in case the company has a question about the order

Page 112: Check form. **1.** *Computer News*, **2.** with a check or be billed later, **3.** in 6 to 8 weeks, **4.** $16, **5.** $45

◆ Lesson 7 Consumer Materials

Page 113: 1. Boats, **2.** Appliances, **3.** Antiques, **4.** Musical Instruments, **5.** Painting Services, **6.** Pets, **7.** Horses and Equipment, **8.** Hobbies, **9.** Computers, **10.** Camping Supplies

Page 114: 1. E, **2.** H, **3.** I, **4.** A, **5.** C, **6.** D, **7.** L, **8.** K, **9.** F, **10.** B, **11.** G, **12.** J

Page 115: 1. porches, **2.** senior citizens, **3.** estimates, **4.** financing, **5.** 7 P.M., **6.** office buildings, **7.** references, **8.** Monday, **9.** supplies, **10.** $10

Page 116: 1. B, **2.** F, **3.** A, **4.** H, **5.** C, **6.** G, **7.** D, **8.** J

◆ Lesson 8 Consumer Materials

Page 117: 1. H, **2.** A, **3.** G, **4.** B, **5.** C, **6.** D, **7.** F, **8.** J, **9.** I, **10.** E

Page 118: 1. by writing or calling, **2.** studying English, working at the newspaper, yearbook editor, **3.** Possible answers: teachers, former employers, **4.** two

Page 119: 1. dental assistant, **2.** 8:00–4:00, **3.** Medical and dental insurance, paid vacation, **4.** Tuesday–Saturday, **5.** by mail, **6.** He is just beginning a practice. **7.** Possible answers:

Good benefits and salary, office closes early.
8. Possible answers: Have to work on Saturday

Page 120: 1. B, **2.** G, **3.** D, **4.** F, **5.** D
Answers will vary. Check application for
completeness.

◆ Unit 3 Assessment

Page 122: 1. B, **2.** G, **3.** B, **4.** F, **5.** C, **6.** G, **7.** D,
8. H, **9.** A, **10.** H, **11.** D, **12.** J, **13.** D, **14.** H,
15. B, **16.** H

◆ Unit 4 Constructing Meaning

Page 125: Possible answers: **1.** Tom's car is
as old as the hills. **2.** Our cat is as fat as an
elephant. **3.** After shoveling the snow, I was as
cold as an iceberg. **4.** Swimming underwater
was like being in a cool, dark cave. **5.** The
noisy three-year-old swept into the kitchen
like a tornado. **6.** Alex was as hungry as a bear.
7. Gina rode her bike like a turtle climbing up
a steep hill. **8.** The alarm clock sounded like a
cannon exploding.

Page 126: 1. year, **2.** city, **3.** steering wheel, **4.** foot,
5. hive, **6.** book, **7.** artist, **8.** crying, **9.** cold

◆ Lesson 1 Recognizing Character Traits

Page 127: 1. Mimi is angry. **2.** by the character's
actions, **3.** Elaine's opinions matter to Jean. She
is critical. **4.** by what others say about the
character, **5.** The woman is rich. She is in a
hurry. **6.** by the character's appearance, by what
the character says or thinks, by the character's
actions

Page 128: 1. C, **2.** J, **3.** A, **4.** Tom withdrew into
his usual morning shell. Tom sat staring at his
bowl of cereal with the usual tight feeling in his
chest. **5.** G, **6.** D, **7.** J, **8.** If I just didn't need the
money so bad, I'd quit.

Page 129: Possible answers: **1.** proud,
2. extravagant, **3.** pretentious, **4.** a braggart,
5. vain, **6.** by his words, **7.** by his actions

Page 130: 1. D, **2.** G, **3.** B, **4.** G, **5.** C, **6.** J, **7.** D, **8.** F

◆ Lesson 2 Recognizing Character Traits

Page 131: 1. Possible answers: older, demanding,
excitable, **2.** impatient, **3.** annoyed and
impatient, **4.** stronger, determined, **5.** Possible

answers: weak, young, fearful, **6.** glad to stop
rowing, **7.** confused and afraid, **8.** not good at
rowing

Page 132: 1. impatient, **2.** narration, dialogue,
3. high-minded, **4.** dialogue, **5.** sympathetic,
6. dialogue, action, **7.** brave, **8.** narration, action,
9. helpful, **10.** dialogue, **11.** friendly, **12.** action,
narration

Page 133: 1. the mother seal, **2.** determined,
caring, **3.** action, **4.** the fox and the narrator,
5. smart, sly, **6.** narration, **7.** people in the room,
darkness, **8.** frightening, powerful, **9.** narration

Page 134: 1. D, **2.** F, **3.** C, **4.** F, **5.** B, **6.** J

◆ Lesson 3 Identifying Main Idea

Page 135: 1. A typhoon hit the coast of Japan.
2. A typhoon hit with full fury today on the
coast of Japan. **3.** Jack London's career as a
writer began with a "punishment" in grammar
school. **4.** In fact, sledding is even becoming a
popular sport in deserts.

Page 136: 1. The sports car is popular for many
reasons. **2.** B, **3.** The pitcher became the key to
a softball team's success. **4.** J, **5.** The platypus
seemed to be a little bit of everything. **6.** C

Page 137: 1. D, **2.** F, **3.** A, **4.** G

Page 138: 1. A, **2.** G, **3.** B, **4.** G, **5.** C, **6.** G

◆ Lesson 4 Finding the Main Idea

Page 139: 1. stated, **2.** In 14th-century Spain,
men wore false beards that were dyed to match
their clothes. **3.** implied, **4.** Writing Chinese is
difficult because there are so many characters,
and they are so detailed.

Page 140: 1. The first paper money in North
America was playing cards. **2.** Bread and other
cereal grains should be an important part of
people's diets. **3.** Piranhas may be the most
vicious fish known to humans. **4.** Honey has
been used as a medicine for centuries.

Page 141: 1. The banyan tree can grow many
new trunks from its low-hanging branches.
2. The term "Indian summer" refers to a warm
period in the fall that occurs after the first frost.
3. People enjoy watching giant sea turtles lay
their eggs. **4.** Many people think that aging
improves the flavor of tea.

Page 142: 1. D, **2.** J, **3.** D

Answer Key *continued*

◆ Lesson 5 Comparing and Contrasting

Page 143: 1. comparison, **2.** similarly, **3.** contrast, **4.** although, while, **5.** both, **6.** like, but

Page 144: 1. killer bees and killer ants, **2.** Accept any two. Possible answers: Both are aggressive. Both like to kill. Their sting can make people ill, or it can kill people. Both came from other places. **3.** ways of cooling and moisturizing air, **4.** Accept any two. Possible answers: wet mats, mechanical fan, rotary fan, air conditioning, **5.** breeds of dogs that weigh more than 220 pounds, **6. a.** Their weight is made of bone and muscle. **b.** They have a shorter life span than small dogs.

Page 145: 1. the cheetah and the gazelle, Accept any two. Possible answers: **2.** Cheetahs can run faster. Gazelles can dodge and jump. Cheetahs run fast for short distances. Gazelles can run fast for longer periods of time. **3.** the number of words various groups or individuals use, Accept any two. Possible answers: **4.** Adults use 3,000 words. Writers use 6,000 words. Shakespeare used 24,000 words in his plays and poetry.

Page 146: 1. B, **2.** D, **3.** F, **4.** H, **5.** B, **6.** D

◆ Lesson 6 Comparing and Contrasting

Page 147: 1. comparison, **2.** body; skyscraper, **3.** similarity, **4.** steel girders of a skyscraper, **5.** contrast, **6.** onions, **7.** but, **8.** size, color, flavor

Page 148: 1. contrast, **2.** animal voices, **3.** comparison, **4.** a camel and a mule, **5.** comparison, **6.** diamonds, sapphires, rubies, emeralds, **7.** contrast, **8.** life spans of mice, opossums, and birds

Page 149: 1. B, **2.** H, **3.** D, **4.** J, **5.** D, **6.** F

Page 150: 1. comparison, **2.** two ship disasters, **3.** both, **4.** contrast, **5.** how much different groups talk with their hands, **6.** by contrast, **7.** contrast, **8.** light-colored and dark-colored clothing, **9.** on the other hand

◆ Lesson 7 Drawing Conclusions

Page 151: 1. A, **2.** G, **3.** D

Page 152: Possible conclusions: **1.** Boats should stay near port. **2.** People in Galveston should prepare for a hurricane. **3.** People should be ready for the hurricane before midnight. **4.** Residents of the area should have candles and flashlights ready. **5.** Residents should store fresh water. **6.** Flooding may occur. People near the shore should protect against water damage.

Page 153: 1. strength, **2.** A, **3.** different, **4.** C, **5.** radios, **6.** B

Page 154: 1. C, **2.** G, **3.** A, **4.** G

◆ Lesson 8 Drawing Conclusions

Page 155: 1. D, **2.** J, **3.** B, **4.** Each dugout would keep a family safe through the winter until the Pilgrims could build log cabins in the spring.

Page 156: 1. near a fault, **2.** far away from the fault, **3.** less, **4.** more, **5.** less, **6.** more

Page 157: Possible answers: **1.** destroyed, stopped, **2.** brave, adventurous, **3.** white mulberry trees, **4.** they make a pleasant sound

Page 158: 1. B, **2.** G, **3.** D, **4.** G

◆ Lesson 9 Recognizing Cause and Effect

Page 159: 1. Cause: Few people visited the antique shop; Effect: it went out of business; Signal words: as a result, **2.** Cause: The new ski-lift runs at the resort meant less crowding on the slopes; Effect: more visitors flocked to the resort; Signal word: so, **3.** Cause: he realized he had left an important report at home; Effect: Mr. Davis turned the car around; Signal word: because, **4.** Cause: Maria read the biography of Abraham Lincoln; Effect: Maria has been considering a career in government; Signal word: since
Possible answers: **5.** I burned my tongue, **6.** we went to another one, **7.** got an upset stomach, **8.** capsized

Page 160: 1. A, C, **2.** F: Their light bones help some ducks stay afloat. G: Their heavy bones help diving ducks stay underwater. **3.** A, B, **4.** F: Bright colors help drakes attract attention during mating season. G: Drakes are unable to fly after molting season.

Page 161: Possible answers: **1.** Cause: Insects seemed to disappear during winter. Effect: People thought insects died and were reborn in the spring. **2.** Cause: Greenland is buried under thousands of feet of ice. Effect: Only the tops of high mountains can be seen. **3.** Cause: Some people have a bad reaction to aspirin. Effect:

Answer Key *continued*

They cannot take aspirin. **4.** Cause: Dolphins can be trained to do many tricks for audiences. Effect: Dolphins are the star performers in many aquariums.

Page 162: 1. cause, **2.** cause, **3.** effect, **4.** cause, **5.** effect, **6.** effect

◆ Lesson 10 Using Cause and Effect

Page 163: 1. B, **2.** H, **3.** D, **4.** F

Page 164: 1. D, **2.** F, **3.** C, **4.** J

Page 165: Possible answers: **1.** Because Lincoln thought his baby son looked like a tadpole, he called him Tad. **2.** The Florida Keys are surrounded by clear waters, therefore, many divers visit the area. **3.** Eyes are washed constantly, so a person has tears all the time. **4.** In order to learn the secrets fossils hold, scientists study them.

Page 166: 1. D, **2.** G, **3.** C, **4.** F, **5.** C, **6.** H

◆ Lesson 11 Summarizing and Paraphrasing

Page 167: 1. summary, **2.** paraphrase, **3.** paraphrase, **4.** summary

Page 168: 1. C, **2.** H, **3.** D

Page 169: 1. Possible summary: The Dead Sea is unusual because of its high salt content. **2.** Possible paraphrase: The Dead Sea is a lake located between Israel and Jordan. It lies 1296 feet below sea level. The salt content is 270 percent. Seawater is about 35 percent. The Dead Sea has no outlet, so the salt content keeps increasing. A person can easily float, but the salt sticks to the skin and is difficult to remove.

Page 170: 1. B, **2.** C, **3.** F, **4.** J

◆ Lesson 12 Summarizing and Paraphrasing

Page 171: 1. summary, **2.** summary, **3.** paraphrase, **4.** summary, **5.** paraphrase, Number 1 and number 5 should be circled.

Page 172: 1. B, **2.** G, **3.** C

Page 173: Possible paraphrase: Today there are many choices for building materials for houses. For example, some houses can be built of molded concrete, aluminum siding, or plastic. In the past, Old English houses and castles were built of stone. In pioneer America, wood was used. But the oldest building material is brick, which was used by the ancient Egyptians.

Page 174: 1. Possible summary: Dogs are able to lose their excess heat by panting, which allows heat to evaporate from their bodies. They also have extra sweat glands on their paws and noses. **2.** Possible paraphrase: There is a reason why a dog pants. A dog does not have many sweat glands, so it cannot cool itself by sweating. It must cool itself by breathing. When panting, its tongue hangs out to provide a large surface from which heat can evaporate. Most heat is lost by panting, but sweat glands on its nose and paw pads help the dog rid itself of heat.

◆ Lesson 13 Using Supporting Evidence

Page 175: 1. Main idea: The first sentence should be circled. Supporting evidence: The other four sentences in the passage should be underlined. **2.** Main idea: The last sentence should be circled. Supporting evidence: The first and the third sentences should be underlined. **3.** Main idea: The first sentence should be circled. Supporting evidence: The other five sentences in the passage should be underlined.

Page 176: 1. B, **2.** Poison ivy is a weed that contains a poisonous oil. **3.** H, **4.** Fire is one of the oldest ways of measuring the passage of time. **5.** A, **6.** H

Page 177: Possible answers: **1.** Birds build nests in gourds put out by humans. **2.** Sometimes birds build nests under the eaves of houses. **3.** Some birds make nests in planters near skyscrapers. **4.** The Lincoln Memorial is a favorite place to visit. **5.** The Washington Monument offers a view of the city. **6.** The White House tour is an interesting activity. **7.** Tasty sauce from fresh tomatoes forms the base. **8.** An assortment of meats and vegetables helps meet each person's preferences. **9.** Freshly grated cheese is a must.

Page 178: 1. B, **2.** G, **3.** C, **4.** G

◆ Unit 4 Assessment

Page 180: 1. D, **2.** H, **3.** A, **4.** G, **5.** C, **6.** F, **7.** B, **8.** H, **9.** B, **10.** F

Answer Key *continued*

◆ Unit 5 Extending Meaning

Page 183: Answers will vary. Possible answers:
Sight: crimson, glistening, panoramic; We sat on the porch and watched the breathtaking, crimson sunset.
Sound: clamor, whisper, melodic; The melodic strains of the symphony filled the concert hall.
Smell: cinnamon, acrid, floral; The scent of cinnamon greeted us before we even noticed the freshly baked apple pie.
Taste: bitter, spicy, lemon; The mixture of peppers gave the salsa a spicy taste.
Touch: sandpaper, velvet, ice; The cat's tongue felt like sandpaper against his hand.

Page 184: Answers will vary. Possible answers: picnic—summer, family, ants; dog—pet, responsibility, friend; concert—crowds, music, fun; car—repairs, freedom, loan; winter—skating, snowman, blizzard; school—sports, homework, friends
Positive: scent, Negative: odor, stink; Positive: chat, confide, Negative: babble; Positive: cozy, Negative: cramped; Positive: relaxed, laid-back, Negative: lazy; Positive: cautious, Negative: cowardly

◆ Lesson 1 Predicting Outcomes

Page 185: 1. Taylor will refuse the letter and won't know he has been nominated to be president. **2.** You can expect that an earthquake will hit soon. **3.** She will work even harder at her music until she is accepted.

Page 186: 1. B, **2.** H, **3.** B

Page 187: 1. The farmers came to battle the British. **2.** More people gave money to the Red Cross or volunteered their services. **3.** She kept adding to the house until she died.

Page 188: 1. A, **2.** J, **3.** B, **4.** G

◆ Lesson 2 Predicting Outcomes

Page 189: 1. the bust of Washington shows him smiling. **2.** aging the sauce made it taste better.

Page 190: Possible answers: **1.** Place the plant in the pot and add more soil to fill the pot. **2.** Next cut the tomatoes, peppers, mushrooms, and other vegetables into bite-sized pieces. **3.** Wet the car using the water and remove the dirt using the rags or sponges. **4.** Begin painting the wall, starting from the strip and working your way down.

Page 191: 1. a. The climber reaches the top. **b.** The climber dies in the storm. **c.** The climber turns back. **2.** Possible answer: Students may say that since the climber is experienced, he or she would respect the power of nature and turn back. **3. a.** The family has a wonderful day. **b.** It starts to rain, and they go home. **c.** Someone gets lost. **4.** Possible answer: Students may say that the word *seemingly* hints that something will happen, and bad weather is a likely possibility. **5. a.** The presentation is a success. **b.** The presentation is a failure. **c.** The executive becomes too upset to give the presentation. **6.** Possible answer: Students may say that since the executive is well prepared, her presentation will be a success despite the setbacks.

Page 192: 1. A, **2.** G, **3.** B, **4.** H

◆ Lesson 3 Identifying Fact and Opinion

Page 193: 1. opinion; lovely, **2.** opinion; cuddly, will adore, **3.** fact, **4.** fact, **5.** fact, **6.** opinion; everyone should, **7.** opinion; impressive, misleading, **8.** opinion; love, **9.** fact, **10.** fact, **11.** opinion; wonderful, **12.** opinion; without question, all, **13.** fact, **14.** opinion; most unique

Page 194: 1. They shouldn't use this term, however, because the waves have nothing to do with tides. **2.** After all, classical architecture is the best model of harmony and proportion. **3.** The entire passage should be circled. **4.** The entire passage should be circled. **5.** Settlers in cities and villages were wise to name their settlements using the beautiful Native American words. **6.** This novel is his best.

Page 195: Answers will vary. Possible answers: **1.** Soccer involves a lot of running. **2.** Soccer is too strenuous for anyone over 20. **3.** *Gone with the Wind* starred Clark Gable. **4.** *Gone with the Wind* is not as good as *Citizen Kane*. **5.** Most watermelons have a green outer covering. **6.** Seedless watermelons taste better than those with seeds. **7.** Fall comes after summer. **8.** Fall is the most beautiful season of the year. **9.** Abraham Lincoln was president during the Civil War. **10.** James Madison was the best president.

Page 196: 1. A, **2.** D, **3.** G, **4.** H, **5.** B, **6.** D, **7.** F, **8.** H, **9.** A, **10.** D

Answer Key *continued*

◆ Lesson 4 Identifying Fact and Opinion

Page 197: 1. fact, **2.** opinion; valid, **3.** opinion; biased, **4.** fact, **5.** opinion; valid, **6.** opinion; biased

Page 198: 1. Cole Porter, an American song writer, was so depressed by the failure of his first musical that he joined the Foreign Legion. **2.** Historians have been unable to verify the popular legend that Betsy Ross made the first flag at the request of a special committee that included General George Washington. **3.** Many people have heard of the Baseball Hall of Fame, which is located in Cooperstown, New York. In the 1970s, a special committee was set up to consider admitting players from the Negro Leagues. **4.** Marian Anderson was a famous African-American singer of her day. One of her most famous concerts took place in front of the Lincoln Memorial.

Page 199: Answers will vary. Possible answers: **1.** "America the Beautiful" is sometimes sung in place of the national anthem. **2.** "America the Beautiful" is the best of all our patriotic songs. **3.** Yellowstone Park is a favorite vacation destination of many people. **4.** Yellowstone Park is the most beautiful of all our national parks. **5.** Ford is one of the oldest American car companies. **6.** A classic car from the 1950s is the perfect car. **7.** Becoming a doctor takes several years of school and training. **8.** Everyone would love being a fashion model. **9.** Dachshunds were once hunting dogs. **10.** Dachshunds are cute little bundles of energy.

Page 200: 1. A, **2.** D, **3.** G, **4.** H, **5.** B, **6.** D, **7.** G, **8.** J, **9.** A, **10.** C

◆ Lesson 5 Recognizing Author's Purpose

Page 201: 1. story, **2.** joke, **3.** newspaper, **4.** newsmagazine, **5.** ad, **6.** letter to the editor, **7.** store catalog, **8.** travel brochure, **9.** recipe, **10.** textbook

Page 202: 1. C, **2.** G, **3.** B, **4.** F, **5.** D, **6.** H, **7.** B

Page 203: 1. a recipe, **2.** to explain or instruct, **3.** a short biography or a report, **4.** to inform, **5.** a letter to the editor or town council, **6.** to persuade or express an opinion, **7.** some jokes, **8.** to entertain, **9.** a descriptive article, **10.** to describe or to inform

Page 204: 1. to inform, **2.** to persuade or express an opinion, **3.** to explain or instruct, **4.** to describe, **5.** to entertain, **6.** to inform

◆ Lesson 6 Identifying Author's Purpose

Page 205: Answers will vary. Possible answers: **1.** to entertain, **2.** to describe, **3.** to inform, **4.** to explain or instruct, **5.** to persuade or express an opinion, **6.** to describe, **7.** to persuade or express an opinion, **8.** to explain or instruct, **9.** to explain or instruct, **10.** to inform, **11.** to describe, **12.** to entertain

Page 206: 1. to explain or instruct, **2.** to inform or to explain, **3.** to persuade or express an opinion, **4.** to describe, to entertain, or to inform, **5.** to entertain, **6.** to persuade or express an opinion

Page 207: 1. entertain, **2.** explain or instruct, **3.** describe, **4.** persuade or express an opinion, **5.** inform, **6.** explain or instruct, **7.** entertain, **8.** inform or describe, **9.** persuade or express an opinion, **10.** describe

Page 208: 1. B, **2.** F, **3.** D, **4.** H, **5.** D, **6.** H, **7.** C

◆ Lesson 7 Recognizing Author's Point of View

Page 209: 1. positive, **2.** stated, **3.** negative, **4.** stated, **5.** negative, **6.** implied, **7.** positive, **8.** implied

Page 210: 1. D, **2.** F, **3.** D, **4.** G

Page 211: 1. positive, **2.** best, **3.** positive, **4.** most peace-loving ever known, **5.** negative, **6.** sly, boasting, cruel, **7.** positive, **8.** Many people have fled to Cape Cod or Martha's Vineyard. The city isn't crowded and getting around is easy. **9.** negative, **10.** difficult, unhealthy, rotten, rancid, cramped, **11.** negative, **12.** Perhaps such an award should be established for our current "professional" baseball team. The award might inspire—or embarrass—the players into better performances.

Page 212: 1. C, **2.** H, **3.** D, **4.** H

◆ Lesson 8 Identifying Author's Point of View

Page 213: 1. dull, **2.** cramped, **3.** old, **4.** cheap, **5.** stubborn, **6.** garish, **7.** bookish, **8.** skinny, **9.** odd, **10.** difficult, **11.** shining, **12.** well-fed,

Answer Key *continued*

13. frugal, **14.** well-used, **15.** ignorant, **16.** refreshing, **17.** controlled, **18.** cabin, **19.** determined, **20.** helpful

Page 214: 1. B, C, **2.** C, **3.** The author's point of view is not valid. Much of what is presented as fact is actually opinion. **4.** The passage presents only one point of view. **5.** The author's point of view toward women's speaking voices is negative.

Page 215: Answers will vary. Possible answers: **1.** The food at Cafe Main Street is delicious, exciting, and original. A trip to this neighborhood restaurant is definitely recommended. **2.** The food at Cafe Main Street is greasy, cold, and expensive. A trip to this neighborhood restaurant is to be avoided. **3.** Congressman Joseph is a hard-working, wise, thoughtful politician. He should be reelected this fall. **4.** Congressman Joseph is a mean-spirited, uninspired, out-of-touch politician. He should not be reelected this fall. **5.** To many people, the most important part of a pizza is the crust. Those who like thin crust will get a pizza with a crisp, crunchy feel in the mouth. **6.** To many people, the most important part of a pizza is the crust. Those who like thin crust will get a pizza that feels hard and tastes like cardboard.

Page 216: 1. C, **2.** H, **3.** B, **4.** F

◆ Lesson 9 Making Generalizations

Page 217: 1. X, **2.** X, **3.** X, **4.** leave blank, **5.** X, **6.** X, **7.** X, **8.** leave blank, **9.** X, **10.** leave blank, **11.** X, **12.** X

Page 218: 1. Usually, diseases affect only a few people in a limited area. **2.** Few monster stories have staying power that matches that of the Loch Ness monster. **3.** Almost everyone has seen some movie in which a thirsty desert traveler thinks he or she sees a pool of cool water in the distance and then finds that he or she has imagined it. **4.** Most experts believe there can be no question how such animals died. *or* Plant eaters became the source of food for other animals. **5.** It goes without saying that there are many ordinary things we can do on Earth that are impossible to do in outer space. **6.** Many people in the United States buy Buick cars, and many people also bathe in Buick bathtubs.

Page 219: Answers will vary. Possible answers: **1.** Many minor characters are as interesting and worthy of study as major characters. **2.** Typically, television programs and movies end happily. **3.** Many people were concerned about the fact that the bald eagle was in danger of extinction. **4.** Many older animals that are under stress will resort to attacking humans.

Page 220: 1. C, **2.** J, **3.** A, **4.** F

◆ Lesson 10 Identifying Style Techniques

Page 221: 1. B, **2.** F, **3.** C, **4.** J

Page 222: 1. Author B, **2.** Author C, **3.** Author E, **4.** Author A

Page 223: 1. descriptive details, **2.** Possible answer: He trudged through the sloppy mess, looking for the warmth and comfort of food and a clean bed. **3.** long sentences, **4.** Possible answer: This was a mystery I would have to ponder and either solve through observation or just ask Mom. **5.** dialogue, **6.** "You ought to try the Internet, Mom. You might like it. And you might let me stay up later," I teased.

Page 224: 1. C, **2.** J, **3.** C, **4.** G, **5.** C, **6.** J, **7.** B

◆ Lesson 11 Identifying Genre

Page 225: 1. nonfiction, **2.** drama, **3.** drama, **4.** fiction, **5.** nonfiction, **6.** nonfiction, **7.** poetry, **8.** fiction, **9.** poetry, **10.** drama, **11.** fiction, **12.** poetry

Page 226: 1. nonfiction, **2.** drama, **3.** poetry, **4.** fiction, **5.** nonfiction, **6.** poetry, **7.** fiction, **8.** drama, **9.** nonfiction, **10.** poetry

Page 227: 1. nonfiction, **2.** drama, **3.** poetry, **4.** poetry, **5.** fiction, **6.** fiction, **7.** drama, **8.** nonfiction

Page 228: 1. Greek myths, **2.** best-selling novel, **3.** short story, **4.** Aesop's fables, **5.** science-fiction story, **6.** editorial, **7.** travel brochure, **8.** science report, **9.** magazine article, **10.** autobiography, **11.** rhyming verse, **12.** song lyrics, **13.** advertising jingle, **14.** haiku, **15.** greeting-card verse, **16.** movie script, **17.** Shakespeare's plays, **18.** comedy script, **19.** school pageant, **20.** TV drama script

Answer Key *continued*

◆ Lesson 12 Applying Passage Elements

Page 229: 1. C, **2.** G

Page 230: 1. C, **2.** J, **3.** B

Page 231: Answers will vary. Possible answers:
1. Endangered species such as elephants and tigers might be good candidates. The farms would be a way to protect and breed them.
2. Most people have used earmuffs or know of them. They are funny things to have invented.
3. If people knew their desserts and salads were made from animal skin and bones, they might not want to eat them.

Page 232: 1. C, **2.** H, **3.** D

◆ Unit 5 Assessment

Page 234: 1. A, **2.** H, **3.** D, **4.** H, **5.** D, **6.** H, **7.** B, **8.** G, **9.** C, **10.** H, **11.** B, **12.** J